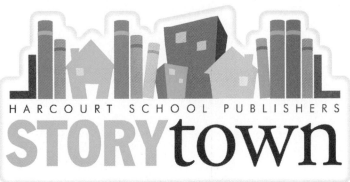

HARCOURT SCHOOL PUBLISHERS

STORYtown

Climbing Higher

Harcourt

SCHOOL PUBLISHERS

www.harcourtschool.com

D1621651

ISBN 0-15-354537-2
ISBN 978-0-15-354537-5

12 13 14 15 16 17 18   1421   16 15 14 13 12 11 10
4500274120

CONTENTS

coincidence

loyal

modeled

murmured

pleasant

recited

Vocabulary

Build Robust Vocabulary

Write the Vocabulary Word that completes each sentence. The first one has been done for you.

Ann and Val were pals. Ann was

(1) _____**loyal**_____ to Val.

Val **(2)** _____ facts in

class. Ann did what Val did.

Ann **(3)** _____ her tan

bag. It was just like Val's bag. What a

(4) _____ !

Ann had to bat. "You can do it!" Ann's dad **(5)** _____ to her. Dad gave Ann a **(6)** _____ pat on the back. Will Ann be like Val now?

Write the answers to these questions. Use complete sentences.

7. Ann had to be like Val. Was this pleasant for Val?

_____

_____

8. Ann's bag was just like Val's. Was this a coincidence?

_____

_____

What a Coincidence!

by Guadalupe V. Lopez

illustrated by Chum McLeod

Ann and Val were pals. Ann was loyal to
Val. Val recited facts. So did Ann. Val was fast.
So was Ann. Ann had to be like Val. **1**

Stop and Think

1 What does Ann do to be like Val?

To be like Val, Ann _____

_____

_____

Val had a tan bag. So Ann had one. Ann modeled her bag. "Look! I have a tan bag!" she said.

Ann had to be like Val. Val did not like this. ❷

Stop and Think

❷ What do we know about Val so far?

I know that Val _____

_____

_____

Val became mad at last. It went like this.

Ann went to hand Val a bat. "Go on. You bat. Then I can bat."

"No! I will not bat. You bat!" Val sat down. She was mad. She did not get up. **3**

Stop and Think

3 Why does Val get mad?

Val gets mad because _____

_____

_____

Now Ann was sad. "What was that for?" She did not get it.

Dad could see Ann was sad. Dad ran to her. He murmured, "See? You are fast. No one will tag you! Go now! You can do it!" ❹

Stop and Think

❹ Find the sentence "She did not get it." What does that sentence mean?

"She did not get it" means _____

_____

Ann was glad Dad said that. She COULD do it! She got her cap. She got the bat. Up she went. She could do it now.

"Come on," said Ann. **5**

Stop and Think

5 How do you think Ann feels now? Why?

I think Ann feels _____

_____

_____

Crack! Look at that! Ann ran. She ran past Sam. She ran past Pam. She ran past Jack. Ann ran so fast. **6**

Stop and Think

6 How can you tell that Ann makes a hit?

I can tell that Ann makes a hit because _____

_____

_____

17

Ann's dad was glad. "Grand slam!" He made a pleasant pat on her back.

Val ran to Ann. "I'm glad I could see that. You are fast!"

Now Ann was glad. "I AM fast. What a coincidence! That's what Dad said!" 7

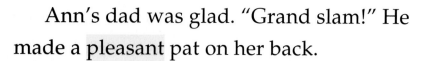

Stop and Think

7 Do you think that Ann will still try to be like Val? Explain your answer.

I think Ann will _____

_____

Think Critically

1. Before Ann made a hit, Val was mad. After Ann hit the ball, how did Val's feelings change? Copy the chart, and fill it in. **CHARACTERS AND SETTING**

Before the Hit	After the Hit
Val was mad at Ann.	

2. Why did Ann's grand slam make Val happy? **CAUSE AND EFFECT**

   Ann's grand slam made Val happy because _____

   _____

   _____

3. If Ann was your friend, how would you feel if she copied you? **MAKE CONNECTIONS**

   If Ann was my friend, I would feel _____

   _____

   _____

assembly

autographed

dismiss

patchwork

plenty

squirmed

Build Robust Vocabulary

Read the story and think about the meanings of the words in dark type.

"I will **dismiss** the class," said Miss Adams. The kids went to the **assembly.** They had **plenty** to do there. They saw a big **patchwork** quilt. They saw Fran Mills. She had her books. Miss Mills **autographed** a book. Hal **squirmed** as he sat. He is a big fan. Will she autograph *his* book?

Write the Vocabulary Word that completes each sentence. The first one has been done for you.

1. Miss Adams will _____ **dismiss** _____ the class.

2. The kids went to the _____ .

3. They saw a _____ quilt.

4. They had _____ to do.

5. Hal _____ as he sat.

6. Miss Mills _____ a book.

Miss Mills

by **Guadalupe V. Lopez**   illustrated by **Bridget Star Taylor**

When will Miss Adams dismiss the class?
Hal can't sit still. There is a big assembly.
The class will go in a bit. They will see Fran
Mills. Hal is a big fan. **1**

Stop and Think

1 What do you know about the story so far?

I know _____

_____

_____

Now they were in the assembly. Hal could not sit still. He squirmed. Then he saw her. "There she is! It's Miss Mills!" ❷

Stop and Think

❷ Find the word *squirmed*. What does this word mean?

The word "squirmed" means _____

_____

_____

"I'm glad you came," said Miss Mills.

"How are you?"

Hal was still. Then his hand went up fast. ③

Stop and Think

③ Hal raises his hand. What do you think will happen next?

After Hal raises his hand, I think _____

_____

_____

© Harcourt

He stands. "I'm Hal. I have *Cabin in the Hills*. I like it! I read it over and over. It's as if I'm there. How did you do it?"

He sits back down. ❹

Stop and Think

❹ What is *Cabin in the Hills*? Underline the words on the page that tell you.

"Cabin in the Hills" is _____

_____

"We had a cabin," said Miss Mills. "I was a kid. Rabbits were out back. They ran all over."

"We went fishing. We had picnics. We had plenty to do." ❺

Stop and Think

❺ What did Miss Mills do at the cabin when she was a kid?

When she was a kid, Miss Mills _____

_____

_____

"I made a patchwork quilt. It has bits of my past. Look at it. See this rabbit? I added this and that. Then the quilt was finished!" **6**

Stop and Think

6 Why does Miss Mills's patchwork quilt have a rabbit on it?

Miss Mills's quilt has a rabbit on it because _____

_____

_____

"It's like *Cabin in the Hills*. It has bits of my past. I added this and that. Then the book was finished! I'm glad you like it!"

Then Miss Mills autographed the book. It was her gift to Hal. **7**

Stop and Think

7 How do you think Hal feels when Miss Mills autographs his book?

I think Hal feels _____

_____

Think Critically

1. What is the setting of this story? What are the story events? Copy the chart, and fill it in. CHARACTERS AND SETTING

```
┌─────────────────┐   ┌─────────────┐
│   Characters    │   │   Setting   │
│    Hal and      │   │             │
│   Miss Mills    │   │             │
└────────┬────────┘   └──────┬──────┘
         │                   │
    ┌────┴───────────────────┴────┐
    │        Story Events         │
    │                             │
    │                             │
    └─────────────────────────────┘
```

2. In what ways is Miss Mills's quilt like her book? MAKE COMPARISONS

   Here are ways they are alike: _____

   _____

   _____

3. What do you think the author wants you to learn from this story? AUTHOR'S PURPOSE

   I think the author wants me to learn _____

   _____

   _____

certain

chores

culture

resources

tutor

uniforms

Vocabulary

Build Robust Vocabulary

Write the Vocabulary Word that completes each sentence. The first one has been done for you.

We get out of bed. We put on our **(1)**

_____**uniforms**_____ to go to class.

We make our beds. We do other

(2) _____ .

We go down the hill to class. We look

at the class list. **(3)** _____

kids are in Miss Ana's class. Some are

not. We will find out.

© Harcourt

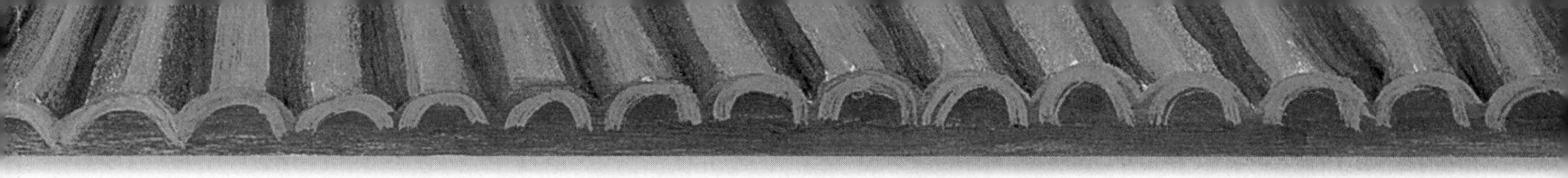

We sing to the flag. It is a song of our

(4) _____ . There are

a lot of **(5)** _____

in our class. We look at the maps.

We add in class. Max can't add fast.

Miss Ana will **(6)** _____

him. Then he will get it.

**Write the answers to these questions.
Use complete sentences.**

7. What chores do the kids do?

_____

_____

8. What resources do you see in their class?

_____

_____

Down the Hill

by Ana Julia Velasco

illustrated by Shelly Bartek

It is six o'clock. Kids have to get up fast. They have to get on their uniforms. They do quick chores. They sip hot milk. They kiss Mom. They kiss Dad. They grab their bags. They have plans. Off they go! ❶

Stop and Think

❶ Where do you think the kids are going? Why?

I think the kids are going _____

_____

_____

The kids go down the hill. They hop over rocks. They skip along the path. They stop to pick up pals.

They are all glad to go. Some will be in this class. Some will be in that one. Certain kids are in Miss Ana's class. Some are not. They will see. They will look at the class list when they get there. They will find out. ❷

Stop and Think

❷ What will the kids do first when they get to school?

First, the kids will _____

_____

_____

They skip down the block. They stop at Miss Liz's stand. She has a box of figs. They are soft and black. Two kids get figs for a snack. Then they all go on.

Stop and Think

3 Who is Miss Liz?

Miss Liz is _____

_____

_____

34

They are there at last. They flock to the list. They stand and look. They find him. They find her. They are all in Miss Ana's class! That is grand! ❹

Stop and Think

❹ How do you find out which class you will be in each year?

Each year, I find out which class I will be in by _____

_____

_____

Into class they go. It has a lot of resources. The kids look at them all. Then they sit down.

Miss Ana is glad to see them. She nods and winks. She has jobs and tasks planned. **5**

Stop and Think

5 What are some of the resources in the class?

Some of the resources are _____

_____

_____

She asks them to stand. They sing to the flag. It's a song of their culture. Then they stop. They sit down.

They look at maps. They find spots on the maps. They add. Tom adds fast. Miss Ana sees that. Max can't get it. So Miss Ana will tutor him. Then Max will get it. **6**

Stop and Think

6 If you wanted to find the meaning of the word *culture*, would you look in the table of contents or the glossary of a book?

I could look _____

_____

Now class is over. The kids get their bags.
They are set to go.

Miss Ana will make the class fun. The kids
like Miss Ana. They all like their class. **7**

Stop and Think

7 How do you think the kids feel now?

I think the kids feel _____

_____

_____

Think Critically

1. How do you know the kids like Miss Ana? Copy the chart, and fill it in. MAIN IDEA AND DETAILS

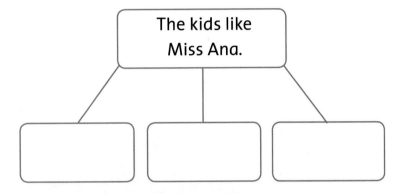

2. How is this school the same as your school? MAKE COMPARISONS

In both schools, _____

_____

_____

3. Why do you think the author chose to write about this school? AUTHOR'S PURPOSE

I think the author wrote about this school because

_____

_____

apply

disappointed

hinder

invention

research

talented

Vocabulary

Build Robust Vocabulary

Write the Vocabulary Word that completes each sentence. The first one has been done for you.

Mae wanted to learn new things. "I will do

(1) _____**research**_____ when I get

big," she said.

Mae said, "You will not be

(2) _____ in me."

Mae was strong. She did not let anything

(3) _____ her.

She finished school. After that, Mae wanted

to (4) _____ for

college. She did well in college.

Then Mae did a lot of jobs. She is

(5) _____ .

In one job, she made something new.

It was an (6) _____

to help sick kids.

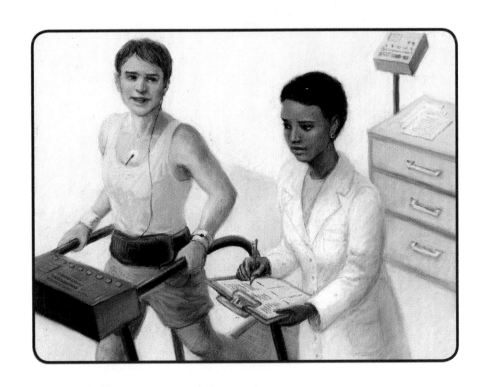

Mae  Jemison

by Cecilia Rosario • illustrated by Lyuba Bogan

"Mae Jemison, you are little now. What will you do when you get big?"

"I'll do research," she said. "I'll learn how to do lots of things. I'll have the best job." She was six. **1**

Mae was in a class like this.

Stop and Think

1 What does Mae want to do when she gets big?

When she gets big, Mae wants to _____

_____

_____

"You will not be disappointed in me," said Mae. "I will do my best!"

Mae was strong. She did not let anything hinder her. ❷

Stop and Think

❷ Do you think Mae was a good student? Explain.

I think Mae _____

_____

_____

Then Mae saw someone act on TV.

"She has skills. She is talented." said Mae. "I bet she gets to go up in a rocket. Can I go up over our planet? Can that be my job? Could I travel up there?"

Mae made a plan. She went to class. She did her best. She finished school. ❸

Stop and Think

❸ What do you think Mae's plan was

I think Mae's plan was _____

_____

_____

Then Mae said, "I want to apply to college. I will become a doctor. Then, I will help the sick get well."

Mae got into college! She was set.

Mae did well in college. Now, she was a doctor. She got a job in Africa. She helped sick people who lived there. ❹

Stop and Think

❹ What did Mae do after she became a doctor?

After she became a doctor, Mae _____

_____

_____

Then Mae got her next big job. She would go into space! She had to go to lots of classes. Then she was set for the trip. She blasted up, up, up in a rocket. Mae felt like one of the planets. **5**

Stop and Think

5 How do you think Mae felt as she went into space?

When Mae went into space, I think she felt _____

_____

_____

In Mae's next job, she invented something grand. Her invention helped the sick get well.

Mae's jobs did not end there.

"I have had the best jobs," she said. "How can I help kids do just as well?" **6**

Stop and Think

6 Mae has had the best jobs. What did she choose to do next?

Because Mae had the best jobs, she _____

_____

Now, Mae talks to kids. She tells them to do their best. She tells you to do your best. What will you be? Make a plan. Then tell someone, "I can do that!" 7

Stop and Think

7 What will you do when you get big? Explain your answer.

When I get big, I will _____

_____

_____

Think Critically

1. What did you learn about Mae Jemison's life? Copy the chart, and fill it in. SUMMARIZE

Childhood	
School	
Adult	

2. Why do you think the author wrote this biography? AUTHOR'S PURPOSE

The author wanted to _____

_____

_____

3. You want to find out more about Mae Jemison's school years. To see if a book has these facts, would you look in the table of contents or in the glossary? LOCATE INFORMATION

To see if a book has these facts, I would look in the

_____

_____

Vocabulary

Build Robust Vocabulary

Write the word that best completes each sentence. The first one has been done for you.

1. Miss Drummond tells the

   _____ **viewers** _____ what they will see.

   uniforms   resources   **viewers**

2. This red bug is _____ on

   concealed   independent   disappointed

   Peg's red top. It's hidden.

3. The bug is red. Peg's top is red. It's called

   _____ .

   invention   research   camouflage

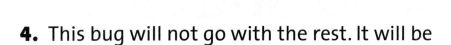

4. This bug will not go with the rest. It will be

_____ .

concealed   independent   donated

5. Mrs. May _____ two boxes

donated   concealed   autographed

of bugs. It's a gift for the class. They will go

on the plants!

6. The bugs get rid of bad insects.
They help the plants. With all the
good bugs, the plant buds will

_____ .

squirm   survive   apply

**Write the answers to these questions.
Use complete sentences.**

7. How can a bug be concealed? _____

_____

8. What helps plants survive? _____

_____

Buds and Bugs

by Guadalupe V. Lopez

illustrated by Marilyn Mets and Peter Ledwon

Cast of Characters

Will	Miss Drummond
Peg	Mrs. May

Will: I am Will. This is Peg. Our class will go on a trip. Miss Drummond, what will we see? Tell our viewers.

Miss Drummond: We will go to Sun Plants Greenhouse to see plant buds and bugs. **1**

Stop and Think

1 Who is going to Sun Plants Greenhouse?

The people going are _____

_____

_____

❶ Who is going to Sun Plants Greenhouse?

_____

_____

Will: Buds and bugs!

Miss Drummond: Yes. It will be fun.

Will: Thank you, Miss Drummond. Let's get on the bus. We are off to Sun Plants! **2**

Stop and Think

2 What does "we are off" mean?

"We are off" means _____

_____

_____

Peg: We are here! The bus trip was fun.

Will: It was not a long trip.

Peg: We sang songs. Will, did you sing?

Will: No, I didn't. But I had fun humming along with you. **3**

Stop and Think

3 What other things could you do on the bus to pass the time?

To pass the time, we could _____

_____

© Harcourt

Peg: Now we are at Sun Plants Greenhouse! This must be Mrs. May.

Mrs. May: I'm glad you could come! There is a lot to see. Look in this box.

Peg: I see hundreds of red bugs! They have little black dots. **4**

Stop and Think

4 Mrs. May says there is a lot to see. Name something the children see.

The children see _____

_____

Mrs. May: Yes, they do. Get this cup. I'll fill it with bugs.

Peg: Now what?

Mrs. May: Let the bugs go on the buds.

Peg: There. I did it. Look at them go!

Will: What do the bugs do, Mrs. May?

Mrs. May: The bugs get rid of bad insects. They help the plants survive. **5**

Stop and Think

5 How do you think the bugs get rid of bad insects?

I think the bugs get rid of bad insects by _____

_____

_____

Mrs. May: Look on your top. Can you see the bug now? It's concealed, or hidden, on all of that red.

Miss Drummond: It's called camouflage. The bug is red. Your top is red. That makes the bug difficult to see.

Will: Maybe this bug is independent. It will not go with the rest of the bugs. **6**

Stop and Think

6 What does the word *top* mean in the sentence "Look on your top"?

In this sentence, the word "top" means _____

_____

Peg: Go do your job, small bug. Go on!

Mrs. May: Miss Drummond, you said the class had some plants?

Miss Drummond: Yes, they do.

Mrs. May: Well, I have a gift. I donated two boxes of bugs. They are for the plants in your class.

Peg: Mrs. May, you are the best! Now our buds will have bugs!

Miss Drummond: Thank you so much.

Will: That ends our trip to Sun Plants Greenhouse. **7**

Stop and Think

7 What do you learn about bugs from this story?

I learn that bugs _____

_____

_____

Think Critically

1. What do you think the children will do with the bugs Mrs. May gave them? **MAKE PREDICTIONS**

I think the children will _____

_____

2. What does the class learn about bugs on their trip? **PLOT**

The class learns that bugs _____

_____

3. Where could you look for more information about plants? **LOCATE INFORMATION**

I could look for more information about plants in

_____

_____

collapses

dazed

elevated

embarrass

midst

shabby

Vocabulary

Build Robust Vocabulary

Read the story and think about the meanings of the words in dark type.

The kids were at their sandlot. It was by the **elevated** tracks. The sandlot was hot and full of dust. Lots of kids played ball there.

Beth swung the bat. It was a good hit! She ran over the **shabby** grass and rocks. Rick grinned at her. She was **dazed** from her run. Rick yelled, "Beth **collapses** when she runs that fast!"

In the **midst** of it all, Seth was having fun. Then Rick said Seth was next. Seth didn't want to **embarrass** himself. But he stepped up.

© Harcourt

Write the Vocabulary Word that completes each sentence. The first one has been done for you.

1. The sandlot was by the

_____**elevated**_____ tracks.

2. Seth was having fun in the

_____ of it all.

3. Rick said Beth _____

when she runs fast.

4. Beth was _____ from

her run.

5. Seth didn't want to _____

himself at bat.

6. The grass at the lot was

_____ .

A Big Fan

by Ana Celia Cervantes
illustrated by A. J. Garces

Beth landed in a puff of dust. She had just run the length of the lot.

"That was a big hit," I said.

Beth grinned and picked herself up. We slapped hands.

Rick yelled, "Beth collapses when she runs that fast. But that was swell! Seth, you are next." ❶

Stop and Think

❶ What did Beth just do? How do you know?

I know that Beth just _____

_____

_____

Our sandlot sat next to the elevated tracks. It had some shabby grass and sand, along with rocks and sticks. In the midst of this, we had fun.

Lots of kids came here. Beth and I were from Fifth Street. Rick came from Tenth Street. And the twins were from the next block. **2**

Stop and Think

2 How do you know the sandlot is in the city?

I know the sandlot is in the city because _____

_____

_____

I went to bat. "Say when," said Rick.

"When!" I yelled back. He whipped it at me. I missed. I was dazed. I stepped back. As I tapped the bat, I could see someone out past the lot. He had a bag.

It was Al Mathis! He hit the best of all. He was thin like a stick. He was swift like the wind. I was his biggest fan. ❸

Stop and Think

❸ What opinion does the storyteller give about Al Mathis?

The storyteller gives the opinion that Al Mathis _____

_____

_____

"Come on, Seth. Let's go," yelled Rick. I propped up my bat.

Al Mathis stopped. He set down his stuff. "Oh, no," I thought. "Now I will embarrass myself." I lifted the bat. I wanted to get just one hit. Al Mathis would see. ❹

Stop and Think

❹ What do you think will happen next?

I think that _____

_____

_____

Wham! My bat connected! It was a hit. I ran like the wind. I made it! I sent a look back at Al. I had hit it past him! He grinned. I felt just fantastic. ⑤

Stop and Think

⑤ Seth says he feels fantastic. How do you think Al feels?

I think Al feels _____

_____

_____

I went over to him. "You're Al Mathis. I'm a big fan of yours."

"Thank you," he grinned. "Let me tell you something. This was my lot long ago. I came to this spot as a kid. And this is the lot I still came to when I made it big."

I said, "Hit some with us." **6**

Stop and Think

6 How are Seth and Al the same? How are they different?

Here is how they are the same: _____

_____

Here is how they are different: _____

"That could be fun," said Al. "But I have to go. That was a big hit."

"Thanks!" I said.

The bus came to a stop. Al got on. He tipped his cap at me. "Thanks for the fun, Seth. I think you'll make it big as well."

I could not help but grin. ⑦

Stop and Think

⑦ What might Al have been thinking as he watched Seth bat?

Al might have been thinking that _____

_____

Think Critically

1. What are two facts and two opinions from the story? Copy the chart, and fill it in. FACT AND OPINION

Fact	Opinion

2. Why is Al Mathis important to the story? PLOT

Al Mathis is important to the story because _____

_____

_____

3. If it was your turn to bat, and Al Mathis was watching, what would you do? PERSONAL RESPONSE

I would _____

_____

_____

© Harcourt

69

demonstrate

obey

patrol

scent

wanders

whined

Vocabulary

Build Robust Vocabulary

Write the Vocabulary Word that completes each sentence. The first one has been done for you.

Champ is a K-9 dog. Mitch is his pal.

Champ and Mitch are on

(1) _____patrol_____ . They fix

problems and help us. That is their job.

Not all dogs can be K-9 dogs. Champ

had to pass a test. Some dogs in Champ's

class **(2)** _____ . They

didn't know what to do.

Champ had to **(3)** _____

what he can do. He had to

see and smell well. Champ will

do what Mitch tells him. He

will **(4)** _____ Mitch.

If someone **(5)** _____

off, Champ can help. He sniffs. He tracks

their **(6)** _____ .

Champ on Patrol

by Guadalupe V. Lopez

illustrated by Erica Pelton Villnave

Champ and Mitch are on patrol. Champ is a K-9 dog. Mitch is his pal.

Champ and Mitch are on the lookout. They fix problems and help us. They do lots of jobs to help people. 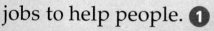 ❶

Stop and Think

❶ Who is Champ? What jobs does he have?

Champ is _____

_____

_____

Not all dogs can be K-9 dogs. Champ had to pass a test. Lots of dogs were in the class. Some of the dogs whined when they didn't know what to do. Some did not obey. Some snapped and barked a lot. They didn't pass the test. They could not be K-9 dogs.

But Champ passed. He was the best! That's when he went to Mitch. **2**

Stop and Think

2 Will Champ be a good partner for Mitch? Explain.

I think Champ _____

_____

_____

73

Mitch is glad to have Champ. Champ has strong legs. The dog thinks fast. He runs fast. He can jump over things. He can see and smell well.

Champ will do what Mitch tells him to do. He will sit still when Mitch asks. The dog will do his patrol job well. **3**

Stop and Think

3 Mitch is glad to have Champ. Write three reasons why.

Mitch is glad to have Champ because _____

_____

_____

What happens if someone like you wanders off? You may get lost! Your mom will be upset. She can't see you. What will she do?

Mitch tells Mom to get your jacket. Champ sniffs it. It smells like you. Champ tracks your scent. Mitch and Mom go with Champ.

Then the dog sees you! You see Champ and then your mom. You are glad to be back with your mom. She's glad, too. Champ is such a helpful dog. **4**

Stop and Think

4 What opinion does the author give about Champ?

This is an opinion about Champ: _____

_____

_____

What if someone takes a bag and runs off? Champ and Mitch demonstrate their moves. "Catch that man!" commands Mitch. Champ jumps out. The man sees Champ. But he is no match for this fast dog. Champ does his job well. **5**

Stop and Think

5 What does it mean when someone "runs off"?

When someone "runs off," it means _____

_____

_____

Mitch and Champ visit sick children. The children ask, "Can Champ catch?"

"Can Champ sit up?"

"Can Champ sing?"

Champ shows what he can do. No, he can't sing, but the kids are still impressed.

"Can I hug Champ?" asks one.

"You must always ask first. So thank you for asking," Mitch tells him. "But it's best not to hug him. You can scratch his chin. He likes to be scratched." **6**

Stop and Think

6 If you could meet Champ and Mitch, what would you ask them?

I would ask _____

_____

Mitch and Champ go on patrol. They do a lot. They help lost children. They look out for problems. They visit sick children.

Now, Mitch sits to rest. Champ rests with him. He looks up at Mitch. Mitch scratches Champ's chin. They are best pals.

Champ looks as if he is thinking, "When is lunch? I'll split a chicken sandwich with you, Mitch." **7**

Stop and Think

7 What does the author want you to understand about patrol dogs?

The author wants me to understand that _____

_____

Think Critically

1. What are two facts you learned about Champ? What are two opinions? Copy the chart, and fill it in.
FACT AND OPINION

Fact	Opinion

2. How are Mitch and Champ the same? How are they different? COMPARE AND CONTRAST

These are ways Mitch and Champ are the same:

_____

_____

These are ways they are different: _____

_____

_____

3. Did the author write this selection to make you laugh or to give you facts? AUTHOR'S PURPOSE

The author wrote this selection to _____

_____

Vocabulary

alert

chatter

communicate

flick

grooms

signal

Build Robust Vocabulary

Read the selection and think about the meanings of the words in dark type.

Cluck Cluck

Pets can talk. They can **communicate.** Your dog may bark. It wants to **alert** you.

Your cat hisses. It may arch its back. This is a warning **signal.**

A hen talks fast. It **chatters.** What is the hen telling you?

A pig **flicks** mud all over. Is this to **groom** itself? What is the pig telling you?

Write the Vocabulary Word that completes each sentence. The first one has been done for you.

1. A hen _____ chatters _____ . It talks fast.

2. Pets can _____ . They can talk.

3. A cat gives a warning _____ .
It arches its back.

4. A dog barks to _____ you.

5. A pig may want to _____ itself.

6. It _____ mud all over.

Pets Tell Us

by Guadalupe V. Lopez

Pets are smart. They can talk.
They can communicate. How?
What can they want? Let's see. **1**

Stop and Think

1 What do you think you will learn from this selection?

I think I will learn _____

_____

_____

The yard is dark. A dog barks.
It snarls. What is that dog telling us?

"What is out there?
Is it a cat? I must **see**.
Let me go into the garden!" **2**

Stop and Think

2 How does a dog communicate?

A dog communicates by _____

_____

_____

A cat arches its back. It hisses.
It spits. What is that cat telling us?

"*I want you to* **stop!**
This is a warning signal.
This is my alarm.
I can harm you." **3**

Stop and Think

3 If you see a cat arching its back, why shouldn't you play
with it?

I shouldn't play with it because _____

_____

A hen chatters. It walks tall. It talks fast.
What is that hen telling us? **4**

Cluck
Cluck

Stop and Think

4 How does a hen communicate?

A hen communicates by _____

_____

_____

"Look in the **barn**. There is a small egg. **It is still warm.** I did that!" ⑤

Stop and Think

⑤ How do you act when you do something you are proud of?

When I am proud of something I did, I _____

_____

A pig is in its pen. It is in the mud. It flicks mud all over! What is that pig telling us?

"A mud bath is **fun!** I **like** to fall in it. This is how I grOOm myself." **6**

Stop and Think

6 Why is the pig in the mud?

The pig is in the mud because _____

_____

_____

Watch your pet. It may want to alert you. A pet can have a lot to tell. How will your pet talk to you? **7**

Stop and Think

7 What else do you think a pet can tell you?

I think a pet can tell me _____

_____

_____

Think Critically

1. What do you learn about the ways pets communicate? Copy the chart, and fill it in.

MAIN IDEA AND DETAILS

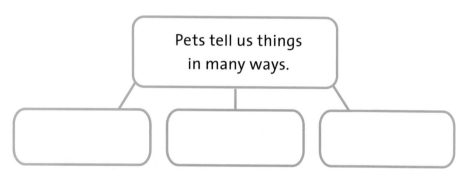

Pets tell us things in many ways.

2. How do dogs and cats communicate when they are happy? USE PRIOR KNOWLEDGE

When they are happy, _____

_____

_____

3. What does the author ask you to do now that you have read the story? Why? AUTHOR'S PURPOSE

The author asks me to _____

_____

_____

agreeable

banquet

curiosity

famine

gaze

generous

Vocabulary

Build Robust Vocabulary

Read the story and think about the meanings of the words in dark type.

In the past, a **famine** had hit the village of Sanborn. The villagers had lost all their crops. But now they were rich in crops. They worked so hard that no one had time to talk or have fun.

Fred had a plan. He planned to be **generous.** He went to the park with a big pot of chicken. He wanted to have a **banquet.**

Pat was walking in the park. He kept his **gaze** down. Then he smelled something **agreeable.** He was filled with **curiosity.** "What smells so good?"

Write the Vocabulary Word that completes each sentence. The first one has been done for you.

1. Sanborn had been hit by a

_____ **famine** _____ .

2. Fred wanted to have a _____ in

the park.

3. Fred planned to be _____ with

his chicken.

4. Pat kept his _____ down as

he walked.

5. Then Pat was filled with

_____ .

6. Pat smelled something

_____ .

More, More

by Guadalupe V. Lopez

illustrated by Donald Wu

Long ago, a famine hit the village of Sanborn. The villagers lost all their crops. But that was the past. Now, things were good again.

Still, the villagers worked so hard. No one made time to talk or have fun. From morning until dark, they did chores on their farms. ❶

Stop and Think

❶ Why do you think the villagers don't talk or have fun?

I think they don't talk or have fun because _____

_____

_____

No one wanted to talk. No one wanted to have fun. Fred sat on his porch thinking about this problem. He had to do something!

So Fred came up with a plan. He made lemon chicken in a big pot, and it smelled so good. He went to the park with his pot of chicken. The smell filled the park. ❷

Stop and Think

❷ What do you think Fred is hoping will happen next?

I think Fred is hoping that _____

_____

_____

Pat walked past the park. He kept his gaze down as he walked. But then, Pat smelled something agreeable. It was the smell of the chicken, and he adored chicken. He looked up, and there was Fred with his pot.

"What is that?" Pat asked with curiosity.

Fred said, "There's a picnic at four o'clock! Do not forget. Why don't you bring something?" **3**

Stop and Think

3 Why do you think Pat keeps his gaze down as he walks?

I think he keeps his gaze down because _____

_____

_____

"I can bring a little corn," said Pat.

"No, no! More, more!" said Fred. "You must bring a lot of corn. Be generous. Get some from your garden."

"I'll do as you ask. I won't forget," said Pat. "I will get lots of corn." So Pat picked corn from his garden and came back to the park. He set his corn next to the big pot. 4

Stop and Think

4 How does Pat show he is generous?

Pat shows he is generous when he _____

_____

_____

Then Lee walked past the park. He could not miss the smell of the chicken. He could not miss the big plate of corn. He could see that Fred and Pat were talking and having fun.

"What is this?" Lee asked.

Fred smiled. "There is a picnic at four o'clock! Can you bring something?" **5**

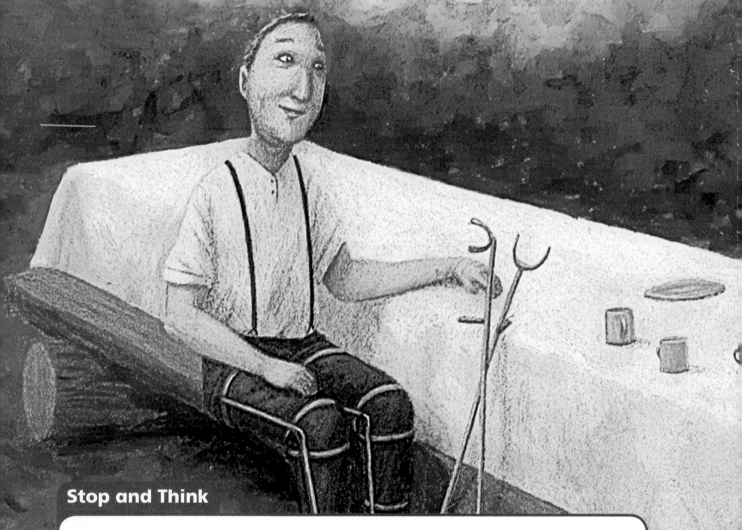

Stop and Think

5 Think about Fred's plan now. Do you think his plan is working? Explain.

I think Fred's plan _____

_____

"I can bring a little milk," said Lee.

"No, no! More, more!" said Fred. "You must bring lots of milk. Get some at the store if you have to."

"I'll do as you ask," said Lee. "I will get lots of milk."

So Lee went to the store and got lots of milk. Then he came back to the park. **6**

Stop and Think

6 How does Lee show he is generous?

Lee shows he is generous when _____

_____

_____

More and more villagers came to the park. Each wanted to bring something to the picnic. It became a grand banquet. The villagers began to have fun.

Then Fred said, "I made a plan to get us talking. My plan worked. Now we can have fun again!"

The villagers clapped and let out a roar. Everyone said that Fred's plan was just grand. **7**

Stop and Think

7 How do you know that Fred's plan solved the problem in the story?

I know that Fred's plan solved the problem because _____

_____

© Harcourt

Think Critically

1. The villagers had fun at the banquet. How can you tell? Copy the chart, and fill it in. **MAIN IDEA AND DETAILS**

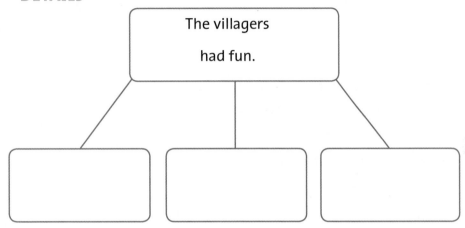

The villagers had fun.

2. Do you think what Fred did was important? Explain your answer. **MAKE JUDGMENTS**

I think what _____

_____

3. How does the author use this story to teach you a lesson? **AUTHOR'S PURPOSE**

The author uses this story to teach me _____

_____

_____

Vocabulary

Build Robust Vocabulary

Write the word that best completes each sentence. The first one has been done for you.

1. Robin and Chip _____**investigate**_____ .

       confess   investigate   suspect

They will find out the truth.

2. The two pals are _____

       experts   alert   laboratory

on puzzles. They are the best!

3. Cat does not think that Egg Meg fell. Cat

says, "I _____ she was pushed!"

    suspect   generous   flick

4. What could have happened to

Egg Meg? Chip and Robin look for

_____ hints.

various   expert   shabby

5. They bring samples back to their

_____ . They will test them.

banquet   assembly   laboratory

6. Maybe a big splash made her fall.

"I _____ I didn't think

chatter   confess   dismiss

of that," said Cat.

Write the answers to these questions.

Use complete sentences.

7. What do Robin and Chip investigate with Cat?

_____

_____

8. Where do you think their laboratory is?

_____

_____

Egg Meg

by Guadalupe V. Lopez

illustrated by David Clar

Cast of Characters

Narrator	Cat
Robin	Muffin Man
Chip	

Narrator: It is ten o'clock in the morning.

Robin: I am Robin and this is Chip. We investigate problems and can find things out.

Chip: Yes. We are the experts on puzzles.

Narrator: A cat dashes in. He looks upset.

Cat: Oh, my! Oh, my!

Robin: What is it, Cat? Do you have a problem? Can we help? **1**

Stop and Think

1 How does Cat feel? How can you tell?

Cat feels _____

_____

_____

Cat: My pal, Egg Meg, sat on a wall. Then she had a bit of a fall!

Robin: Is that so?

Chip: How can we help?

Cat: I suspect she was pushed!

Narrator: Robin and Chip are shocked.

Cat: Can you find out? **2**

Stop and Think

2 In the sentence "I suspect she was pushed," does *suspect* mean a person or something a person does?

In this sentence, "suspect" means _____

_____

Robin: We will find out! But what makes you think she was pushed?

Cat: She couldn't just fall! Could she?

Robin: Let's go. We will look into it.

Chip: We can look for various hints. Lots of hints will tell us what happened.

Robin: Yes. Let's bring our kit. Get some bags. We may have to bring samples back to our laboratory.

Cat: I have to go tell my pals! I must tell them what happened to Egg Meg. ❸

Stop and Think

❸ Why does Robin tell Chip they should take their kit?

Robin tells Chip they should take their kit because _____

_____

_____

Robin: There is Egg Meg. It looks as if she did fall.

Chip: I see a crack in her shell. But it's small. And she's not crushed. How could this have happened? ❹

Stop and Think

❹ **What do you know about Egg Meg's fall?**

I know that Egg Meg _____

_____

_____

Robin: Hmm. Maybe a fish made a big splash. The water then crashed into Egg Meg and pushed her off the wall.

Chip: Maybe. But this wall is tall. A splash of water can't go that far.

Robin: What do *you* think happened? **5**

Stop and Think

5 What do you think will happen next?

I think _____

_____

_____

Chip: I think a gust of wind pushed her.

Cat: Well, I confess I didn't think of that. What now? Egg Meg will want some help.

Narrator: A man comes up to them.

Muffin Man: I can help. I'm the Muffin Man. My shop is over there. This strip of cloth will patch her up! There. How is that? ❻

Stop and Think

❻ If a gust of wind pushed Egg Meg off, was it a strong wind or a soft wind?

A gust of wind is _____

_____

Cat: That will protect her shell. But she needs a safe home.

Narrator: Now the man thinks of a plan.

Muffin Man: Egg Meg can sit on a shelf in my shop. I think she looks dashing!

Cat: Yes, I think she looks grand. Why, Egg Meg, you are blushing.

Muffin Man: I've got it! I'll make a muffin called the "Egg Meg Snack."

Chip: Yum! I want one.

Robin: Make that two!

Narrator: And now that is it. The problem is fixed. ❼

NEW, FRESH "EGG MEG" SNACK

Stop and Think

❼ The Muffin Man says Egg Meg looks dashing. Is this a fact or an opinion? Why?

It is _____

_____

Think Critically

1. What problem does Cat have in the story? How is the problem solved? **PLOT**

Cat's problem is _____

_____

2. How will Egg Meg's life be different in the shop? How will it be the same? **COMPARE AND CONTRAST**

Egg Meg's life will be different because _____

_____

_____

It will be the same because _____

_____

_____

3. Did the author write this story to give information about eggs, or to tell a story about a special egg? **AUTHOR'S PURPOSE**

The author wrote this story _____

_____

_____

brief

chuckling

encouraging

praised

sobbed

soothing

Vocabulary

Build Robust Vocabulary

Write the Vocabulary Word that completes each sentence. The first one has been done for you.

Chad made a short bow. It was a

(1) _____**brief**_____ bow for his fans.

He had made a grand slam. "Outstanding job,

Chad!" his dad **(2)** _____ .

Dad grinned at Jim. "Get set. You are up next!"

Dad was **(3)** _____ to himself.

He was having fun.

"Go for it, Jim! Give it your best!" Dad was

(4) _____ Jim to bat. But

Jim didn't want to bat.

Jim **(5)** _____ . His dad

didn't know why he was sad. Jim's mom sat by

him and rubbed his back. This felt

(6) _____ to him.

Write the answers to these questions. Use complete sentences.

7. What would you praise someone for?

_____

_____

8. What are you doing if you are chuckling?

_____

_____

Proud of You

by Susan McCloskey

illustrated by David Opie

The bat made a loud *crack*! Chad pounded the ball. Dad shouted, "It's past the stands!"

The crowd roared. All the fans jumped up and down. It was a grand slam! The Scouts would get four runs on one hit.

"How is that for good batting!" Mom said.

Chad got back to the bench. He made a brief bow to the fans. Mom, Dad, and Jim crowded around him. "Outstanding job, Chad!" Dad praised. "We are so proud of you!" ❶

Stop and Think

❶ What is a grand slam? How do you know?

A grand slam is _____

_____

_____

"Now the score is four to four," said Mom.

"Yes!" said Dad. "This is the last inning. There are no outs. If our town gets just one more run, we will win!"

Jim frowned. "No!" he said.

Mom put her hand on his arm. "Why do you say that?"

Jim looked down at the ground. Then he looked at Mom. But he didn't want to tell her what he was thinking. ➋

Stop and Think

➋ What do you think Jim is thinking?

I think that Jim is _____

_____

_____

113

Just then, the crowd let out a loud shout. Mel was hit by a bad pitch. Ouch! He ran to first.

Now the fans were shouting, "One more run! One more run!"

Josh stepped up to bat. He missed the first pitch. He hit the next pitch. The ball went up, up, up. Then, down it fell, right into a mitt. There was a shout. "One out!"

Now, Jack was at bat. The first pitch was good. But Jack missed.

"One more run!" the crowd kept shouting.

Jack stepped into the next pitch. He hit the ball. It skipped over the ground and out. It was a foul ball!

Then, came the next pitch. Jack hit it right into the mitt of the kid on first. Two outs! ❸

Stop and Think

❸ Who made the first out? How?

The first out was made by _____

_____

_____

Dad grinned at Jim. Chuckling, he said, "Get set. You are up next! Go for it, Jim! Give it your best! If you get a run, the Scouts will win."

Jim frowned. He looked at his dad. Then he sobbed and ran away from the bench.

Dad didn't know what to think. He asked Mom, "Why did he do that?"

Mom said, "I'll find out." 4

Stop and Think

4 What do you think Jim is feeling right now? Why?

I think Jim is feeling _____

_____

_____

Mom looked for Jim. She found him in back of the stands. He was sitting on a bench. He was still frowning. In the background, the crowd was shouting, "One more run! One more run!"

Mom sat down next to Jim. She rubbed his back with her hand. It felt soothing to him.

"Why so sad?" Mom asked. ❺

Stop and Think

❺ Why is the crowd shouting "one more run"?

The crowd is shouting "one more run" because _____

_____

_____

"Mom," said Jim. "You and Dad are proud of Chad. I want you to be proud of me, too. But I can't hit well. Dad expects me to get a run! What if I make an out?"

Mom said, "He was just encouraging you. He wants you to do your best. He wants you to have fun! That's what counts. So what if you can't hit as well as Chad? He can't play chess as well as you. It's still fun for him. Like this is fun for you."

Jim stopped frowning. "So it's all right to make an out?" he asked.

"Yes," Mom said. "It is. We will still be proud of you!" **6**

Stop and Think

6 What is the problem in the story?

The problem in the story is _____

_____

_____

"Good!" Jim said. He felt proud. "Now, let's go back. I've got a ball to hit."

Jim stepped up to bat. All around was the sound of the crowd. They were shouting, "One more run! One more run!"

Jim could see Mom and Dad. "Yes!" Dad said, clapping his hands. Jim grinned. Mom was right. Come what may, it was fun to play ball. And after all, he *could* get a hit and make the winning run. ❼

Stop and Think

❼ How do you think Jim feels now? Why?

I think Jim feels _____

_____

_____

118

Think Critically

1. What does Jim think will happen if he does not make a good hit? CAUSE AND EFFECT

Jim thinks _____

_____

2. What happened in the story? How was the problem solved? Copy the chart, and fill it in. PLOT

> **Important Events**
>
> ↓
>
> **Solution**

3. What lesson do you think the author wants you to learn from this story? AUTHOR'S PURPOSE

I think the author wants me to learn that _____

_____

_____

din

dodging

heaving

repairs

translate

Build Robust Vocabulary

Read the story and think about the meanings of the words in dark type.

Max's letters were in Spanish. Jennifer counted on her sister to **translate** them. Jennifer had planned for Max to visit over the summer.

Then one morning, a letter came from Max. Max said that a big storm had come. It turned out to be a very **bothersome** storm. Max wrote, "Claps of thunder made a loud **din.** The river ran over the banks. It was **heaving** up rocks. Now we must plant new crops and make **repairs.** That's why I can't visit you."

Jennifer went to the playground. She was thinking of Max as she was **dodging** balls. She wanted Max to visit her. She came up with a plan.

© Harcourt

Write the Vocabulary Word that completes each sentence. The first one has been done for you.

1. Jennifer's sister can _____translate_____ letters from Spanish.

2. Max said the _____ of thunder was loud.

3. The river was _____ up rocks.

4. The storm caused many problems. It was very _____ .

5. Max must help make _____ after the storm. He must fix things.

6. Jennifer was _____ balls at the playground.

Her Pal Max

by Anna McCart

illustrated by Judy Stead

Jennifer and Max sent letters to one another. Max's letters were in Spanish. Jennifer didn't understand Spanish, but her older sister did. Jennifer counted on her sister to translate Max's letters.

Max's letters were interesting. He talked about the farm. It was next to a river. Max swam in the river. Max sent a picture of himself by the river. ❶

Stop and Think

❶ How do you know that Jennifer and Max live far away from each other?

I know that they live far away from each other because _____

_____

Jennifer asked her mom and dad if Max could visit in the summer. "Yes!" they said. Max's parents said yes, too. But his last letter had come in the winter. Now it was summer. There was no new letter from Max. Jennifer was sad. What was the matter? ❷

Stop and Think

❷ How do you think Jennifer felt when her parents agreed to Max's visit?

I think Jennifer felt _____

_____

One morning her sister called out, "Look, a letter from Max!" The letter said what had happened.

"After my last letter, we had a storm. At first it was just a shower. Then the clouds got darker. Claps of thunder made a loud din and the clouds burst. ❸

Stop and Think

❸ Did the clouds get darker before or after the rain shower? Underline the signal words that tell you.

The clouds got darker _____

_____

"The river ran over the banks. It was heaving up rocks. It churned up the dirt and the crops. Now we must plant new crops and make repairs. That's why I can't visit you." ❹

Stop and Think

❹ Why can't Max come to visit Jennifer?

Max can't come to visit Jennifer because _____

_____

_____

Jennifer wondered what to do. Then she remembered her picture of Max.

First, Jennifer cut him out of the picture. She handed the cutout to her dad. "This has to be much, much bigger," she said.

"I'll take it to the shop," Dad said. The picture came back as big as Jennifer!

"Perfect!" said Jennifer. "Now I'll take Max for a visit around town." ❺

Stop and Think

❺ **What do you think Jennifer will do next?**

I think Jennifer will _____

_____

_____

Max and Jennifer had fun in the playground. She had fun dodging a ball while Max watched from the side. Then Jennifer had her sister take a picture of them.

They went to the festival. They had supper at a hot dog stand. They got many pictures.

At last they turned around the corner and walked back to the apartment. Mom snapped another shot. **6**

Stop and Think

6 What is the problem in the story?

The problem in the story is _____

_____

_____

Jennifer sent the pictures to Max. He sent back a letter. It said,

"Thank you for my visit. It was fun. The festival was best of all.

"Packing for a trip is so bothersome. I didn't have to pack for this trip. It's a good thing I had on my best shirt!

"Send me a picture of you. We can have fun here, too. Next summer we'll have another visit, but it will be in person!"

So Mom snapped a shot of Jennifer. She had a big grin. She had on her best shirt. Now it was her turn to visit Max. **7**

Stop and Think

7 If you were Max, how would you feel when you got the photos from Jennifer? Explain your answer.

If I were Max, I would feel _____

_____

_____

Think Critically

1. Why is Jennifer worried at the beginning of the story? CAUSE AND EFFECT

Jennifer is worried because _____

_____

2. What else happened in the story? How was the problem solved? Copy the chart, and fill it in. PLOT

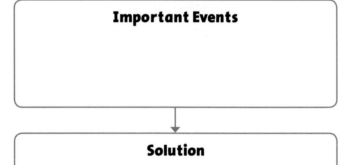

Important Events

Solution

3. How are Jennifer and Max alike? How are they different? COMPARE AND CONTRAST

Here is how they are alike: _____

_____

Here is how they are different: _____

_____

absorb

columns

dissolve

particles

protects

rustling

Vocabulary

Build Robust Vocabulary

Write the Vocabulary Word that completes each sentence in the letters. The first one has been done for you.

Dear Sis,

I'm having fun at Ann's. Her home is next to a big forest.
The trunks of the trees look like big brown

(1) _____columns_____ . They are very tall and thick.

The trees have bark to stop them from getting hurt. The

bark **(2)** _____ the trunk.

The wind makes a **(3)** _____ sound

in the leaves. It's like they whisper to you. I wish you could

be here with me.

Your sister,
Megan

Dear Sis,

I have been helping in the garden. Now I know a lot about plants. Plants must have water and dirt.

Part of the plant is under the dirt. This part can take in water. It can **(4)** _____ the water from the dirt. There are little pieces of things in the dirt. They are called **(5)** _____ . They

(6) _____ in the water. Where do they go? They go in the plant! They help the plant get big and strong.

I like to be in the garden. It's very calm there. You would like it, too.

See you at home,
Megan

Plants

by Molly Fairbrother

illustrated by Gregory Harris

Plants! You can find them all over the globe. This home has lots of plants. It has plants in pots. It has plants in the garden. The yard in back of the home has plants, too. So does the forest next to it. ❶

Stop and Think

❶ What types of plants grow in different places? Use the pictures to help you.

These types of plants grow in different places: _____

_____

One of the plants has red flowers. These are roses. Roses come in many colors. Lots of roses have a fragrant smell. If you see a rose, put your nose close to it. Then take a big sniff.

But watch out for those sharp things on the rose's stem. Those are thorns. Thorns can prick your skin. The thorn protects the rose plant. It says, "Do not come too close! Let me be alone." ❷

Stop and Think

❷ Why do you think a rose plant needs thorns?

I think a rose plant needs thorns because _____

_____

_____

A garden is a good spot to be alone. It's calm here. And some plants can protect you from the hot sun. It's a spot to rest that is not too hot.

A garden is a good spot to be with pals, too. Have a picnic in a garden. Sit on the grass. Look at the different plants, and tell what they are. **3**

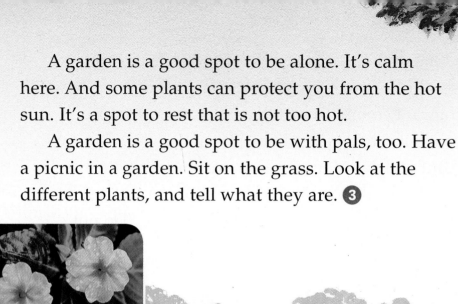

Stop and Think

3 Why is a garden a good spot?

A garden is a good spot because _____

_____

_____

Plants need water. You can water them with a hose or a watering can. Put the hose close to the plants. Let the water drip under them.

Grass is a plant, too. Do not forget to water it! ❹

Stop and Think

❹ What do you think you will learn next?

I think I will learn _____

_____

_____

How does a plant use water? Parts of the plant are under the dirt. These parts absorb water from the dirt. There are particles that dissolve in the water. The water brings these to the plants. They are good for plants. They help plants get big and strong. **5**

Stop and Think

5 Tell how a plant uses water.

A plant uses water to _____

_____

_____

© Harcourt

These plants are the biggest of all. They are trees. Their stems are called trunks. Trunks are covered with bark. Bark protects the trunk. Bark helps animals, too. They can grab onto the bark. It helps them run up to their homes in holes and nests.

Trunks can get very tall and thick. Look down a path in the forest. The tree trunks will look like brown columns. When the wind blows, a rustling sound comes from the leaves. **6**

Stop and Think

6 Why does a tree need bark?

A tree needs bark because _____

_____

_____

© Harcourt

It's fun to watch a plant get big. First, find a spot in the sun. Then, dig a hole in the dirt. Put the root part of a small plant in the hole. Fill the hole with dirt, and add water. You can watch the plant and hope for the best. Take notes on what you see. Watch the plant get big. And don't forget to water! **7**

Stop and Think

7 Why do you think the author tells you how to plant?

I think the author tells me how to plant so _____

_____

_____

Think Critically

1. What have you learned about plants? Copy the chart, and fill it in. MAIN IDEA AND DETAILS

Where They Grow	Plant Parts	Plant Care

2. If a plant does not grow, what might be wrong?
CAUSE AND EFFECT

A plant might not grow if _____

_____

3. How are trees and roses the same? How are they different? COMPARE AND CONTRAST

This is how trees and roses are the same: _____

_____

_____

This is how they are different: _____

_____

_____

©Harcourt

139

glimpse

maze

roost

spears

strikes

suppose

Vocabulary

Build Robust Vocabulary

Read the selection and think about the meanings of the word in dark type.

Suppose you got a **glimpse** into the forest. You would see lots of plants. You would see lots of animals.

The nuthatch bird will **roost** in its nest. It **spears** insects with its beak. The bird will put a bug in the bark of a tree. It **strikes** the bug to crush it. The bird will use the smell of the bug to warn off other animals.

There are ants in the forest. A **maze** of tunnels ties them into one big home.

In the river, you may see some otters. They slide in the mud and ride on their mom's back. There are lots of things to see in the forest.

Write the Vocabulary Word that completes each sentence. The first one has been done for you.

1. A nuthatch _____**spears**_____ insects with its sharp beak.

2. If you get a _____ into the forest, you can see lots of things.

3. There are many paths in an ant's home. Their home is a _____ of tunnels.

4. The nuthatch bird _____ at a bug. It hits the bug hard.

5. The nuthatch bird likes to _____ in a nest.

6. _____ you look into the forest. What would you see?

What Is Inside?

by Susan McCloskey

illustrated by Leland Klanderman

What Is Inside?

There is a hole beside a river. Inside the hole is a den. And inside the den are five otters. One is the mom. The rest are her pups.

Otters are made for swimming! Their back flipper drives them. Their back legs turn them. And their fur helps them glide. They like to swim and dive and, best of all, they like to play! **1**

Stop and Think

1 Why do otters make a den beside a river?

Otters make a den beside a river because _____

_____

_____

Suppose you got a glimpse of the pups. What would you do? Smile! The pups are fun to watch. They have a good time. They ride on Mom's back.

The otters slide in the mud. They toss things. They pretend to hide. Then they run after their brothers and sisters. Life as otter pups is just fine with them! ❷

Stop and Think

❷ What have you learned about otters?

I have learned that otters _____

_____

_____

What Is Inside?

Look inside. Do you see a nest? It has eggs. The eggs will hatch into little birds.

The nuthatch bird likes this nest. It tries to roost in the same nest again and again. It fixes the nest up in the spring. Then it puts the new eggs inside.

This bird tries to catch bugs and flies. It spears the insects with its beak. When it catches them, the bird may not dine on them right away. It may hide the bugs for another time. **3**

Stop and Think

3 Why do you think a nuthatch would not eat a bug right away?

I think a nuthatch would not eat a bug right away because

_____

_____

Sometimes a bird will stuff a bug into a crack in the bark. It strikes with its bill to crush the bug. Then the bird wipes its nest with the crushed bug. The smell says to other animals, "This is mine. Don't come here!"

The bird flies from branch to branch. Look for a flash of white. It could be a nuthatch! ❹

Stop and Think

❹ What animal do you think you will learn about next? Explain your answer.

I think I will learn about _____

_____

What Is Inside?

A hole hides ants. Their nest is under the ground. It has many different parts. A maze of tunnels ties them into one big home.

Ants are not all alike. They come in different sizes and colors. Their nests are different, too. But all ants work hard. They share the work. Different ants do different jobs. ❺

Stop and Think

❺ How do you think ants dig tunnels?

I think ants dig tunnels _____

_____

_____

© Harcourt

Some ants work inside. Some ants spend lots of time outside. They walk around in long lines. They are hunting for things to dine on.

Ants are good at hunting. An ant's mouth has sharp parts. The ant bites with the parts. **6**

Stop and Think

6 How are ants different from each other?

This is how they are different: _____

_____

_____

147

It's dark inside an ant nest. But ants know what jobs to do. They know by smell. Smell tells them where to put their eggs. The smell can tell them if an ant has died inside the nest. Then they rush to take it outside.

Look around. What holes do you see? What is inside them? **7**

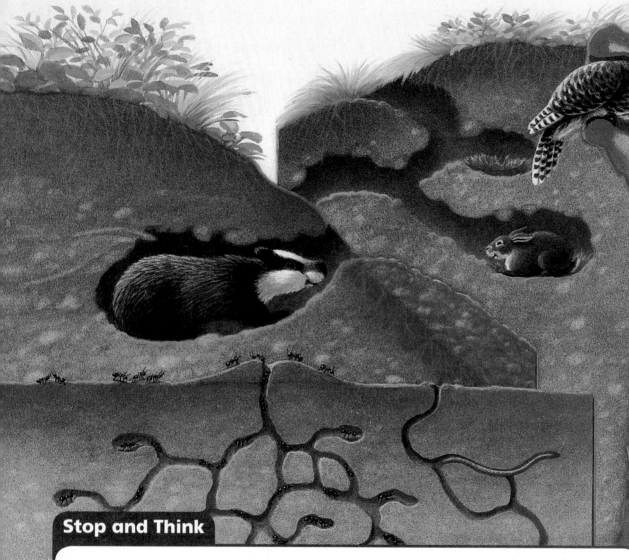

Stop and Think

7 What are some other animals that live in holes? Use the picture to help answer the question.

Some other animals that live in holes are _____

_____

Think Critically

1. What have you learned about animals that live in holes? Copy the chart, and fill it in. MAIN IDEA AND DETAILS

Otter	Nuthatch	Ant

2. How are the animal holes in the story alike? How are they different? COMPARE AND CONTRAST

Here is how they are alike: _____

_____

_____

Here is how they are different: _____

_____

_____

3. What does the author want you to learn from this selection? AUTHOR'S PURPOSE

The author wants me to learn _____

_____

_____

Vocabulary

Build Robust Vocabulary

Write the word that best completes each sentence. The first one has been done for you.

1. We _____**recommend**_____ that you watch

   recommend   devise   translate

   this news report. If you do, you will get

   lots of good tips.

2. The experts will give _____

   repairs   grooms   advice

   on the best things you can do.

3. The reporters _____ with

   recommend   devise   consult

   other kids and adults. They may

   get some good tips.

4. One _____ you may want to
issue   roost   curiosity

know more about is fitness.

5. When is the best time to do homework?

You should _____ a plan
suppose   devise   dissolve

to get it done.

6. Apples, carrots, and milk are

_____ snacks. They are
rustling   sensible   laboratory

not bad for you. That's a good tip.

Write the answers to these questions.
Use complete sentences.

7. Who would you consult if you wanted advice?

_____

8. What issue is important to you?

_____

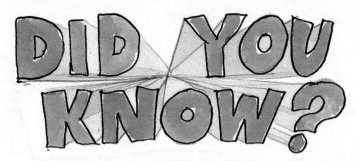

DID YOU KNOW?

by Ernest Kaye • illustrated by Brian Floca

CAST OF CHARACTERS:
Shannon (Newscaster)
Alex (Newscaster)
Will (Fitness Reporter)
Brandon (Science Reporter)
Marisa (Book Reporter)
Robin (Reporter-at-Large)
Chorus

Shannon: Good morning. I am Shannon.

Alex: And my name is Alex. This morning we have something new for you.

Shannon: Our experts will give you advice. **1**

Stop and Think

1 What do the newscasters have for their classmates?

The newscasters have _____

_____

_____

Alex: We asked our reporters to go out into the halls to talk with you.

Shannon: Share with us a subject you would like to know more about.

Alex: We consult with other kids and adults. Their responses can help us help you . . .

Shannon: . . . know the best thing to do! ❷

Stop and Think

❷ What would you like to know more about?

I would like to know _____

_____

_____

Alex: Let's go to our reporter Will. Will?

Will: We have a classmate who wants to know if walking in the halls is good for him. Is it?

Chorus: No! Yes! Maybe!

Will: Well, walking is good for you, but you do not walk far when you just go from class to class. That's why we take time to go outside to run, to walk, and play games.

Chorus: But what does that do for us?

Will: It helps us get in shape. It helps us be more alert. Then we may get better grades! **3**

Stop and Think

3 What may happen if you walk or run and get in shape?

If I walk or run and get in shape, I may _____

_____

_____

Alex: Good advice, Will. There are a lot of activities we can do to get in shape.

Shannon: Let's go to our reporter Brandon.

Brandon: Well, Shannon, we found an interesting subject. Our classmate wants to know why it is important to drink water.

Chorus: Because it stops your thirst!

Brandon: Well, it does. You are made of about 70 percent water. So you must drink water to stay alive. Water also helps you get the dirt off when you take a bath or shower. **4**

70%

Stop and Think

4 Why would water help you stay alive?

Water helps us stay alive because _____

_____

_____

Shannon: I'm amazed that we're made of that much water. Good job, Brandon.

Alex: Let's go to our reporter Marisa.

Marisa: We are at the sports hall. The kids here ask, "When is the best time to do homework?"

Chorus: At home? On the bus?

Marisa: Yes! You can do it after school, too. Many of you do homework before you go to bed. But it could get too late. You must devise a plan for doing your homework before you get tired. **5**

Stop and Think

5 What will happen if you are tired when you do your homework?

If I am tired when I do my homework, _____

_____

_____

Alex: That's a plan, Marisa.

Shannon: Now let's see what Robin has for us.

Robin: Our classmates want to know this. What makes a good snack after school?

Chorus: CHIPS! SOFT DRINKS! CAKE!

Robin: Those snacks have a lot of salt, fat, and sugar. Other snacks are *good* for you. Apples, carrots, popcorn, crackers, and milk are better snacks. **6**

Stop and Think

6 What kinds of good snacks do you eat after school?

The good snacks I eat after school are _____

_____

_____

Shannon: Those are all sensible tips

Alex: We recommend that all our classmates watch our next report.

Shannon: You can find this advice in the latest printed issue of Student News. Ask your teacher.

Alex: Well, back to class. And don't be late! **7**

Stop and Think

7 What do you think the author wants you to learn from this play?

I think the author wants me to learn _____

_____

_____

Think Critically

1. Why do you think the author uses questions and advice from students? **AUTHOR'S PURPOSE**

I think the author does this because _____

_____

_____

2. What are the subjects covered in this report and how do they help us? **PLOT**

The subjects are _____

_____

_____

_____

3. Would you like to see a news report like this in your school? Why or why not? **PERSONAL RESPONSE**

I would _____

_____

_____

brittle

cunning

delighted

disguised

embraced

tender

Vocabulary

Build Robust Vocabulary

Write the Vocabulary Word that completes each sentence in the diary. The first one has been done for you.

Monday, September 4th

This morning, Mom left to go to the store. She said I didn't have to go. I was **(1)** _____delighted_____ by this. I wanted to be at home. Mom gave me a hug. "Do not go into the forest," Mom said as she

(2) _____ me.

The Big Bad Wolf lives in the forest. It's a smart wolf that can trick you. But I'm smart, too. I bet I'm more

(3) _____ than that wolf!

I came out to pick fruit from the garden. I wanted to find a big **(4)** _____ melon. They are so good! But there's no fruit left. I asked Dad why. He said it's because of the strong fall wind. It made the plants **(5)** _____. Their stems are snapping off now.

I am bored. But I didn't tell Dad that. I grinned at him. I **(6)** _____ how I felt. I can't let him see that I'm bored. He will find work for me to do. I would rather play my flute. And I still want some fruit. I bet there's some in the forest. Maybe I can just have a quick look.

Sue and the Big Bad Wolf

by Wiley Gaby

illustrated by Jim Madsen

There was a little girl. Her name was Sue. Sue liked to do many things. She liked to play outside. She liked to pick fruit from the garden. She liked to play tunes on her flute.

Sue grew up in a little blue house. It was next to a huge forest. Her mom and dad had one big rule. "Never go into that huge forest! The Big Bad Wolf lives there." **1**

Stop and Think

1 What does Sue like to do?

Sue likes to _____

_____

_____

Sue stuck to that rule. She never went into the huge forest.

Then that fall Sue's mom went to town. She wanted to get things for stew. But first she said to Sue, "You be safe. Do not go into the forest." Then off Mom went.

After a while, Sue grew bored. Maybe she would play outside. She grabbed her flute. Then she walked into the garden. Maybe she would pick some fruit. But there was no fruit left. The fall wind was too strong. It had made the tender plants brittle. Their stems snapped off as she brushed by. ❷

Stop and Think

❷ What do you think Sue will do next? Why?

I think Sue will _____

_____

_____

Sue made a plan. "There may still be fruit in the forest. I will go in there. Just for a bit."

So Sue walked into the forest. The wind blew hard. Sue shivered. Still she walked on. She didn't see any fruit.

Then out of the blue, a wolf jumped out from the branches and blocked the way. "Little girl!" she growled. "Stop!"

Sue disguised her terror with a smile. "Yes?" she gulped. ❸

Stop and Think

❸ Why does Sue smile even though she is scared?

Even though Sue is scared, she smiles because _____

_____

_____

"Why are you here?"

"I want some fruit. Can you help me?"

"It's my fruit!" the wolf shouted. "Why would I share with you?"

"I'll play you a tune!" offered Sue.

Sue began to play a tune. As she did, the wolf grew tired. Her lids began to close. Soon, she began to snore.

Stop and Think

4 What does Sue want from the wolf?

Sue wants _____

_____

_____

Sue tried to run away. But after a few steps, the wolf woke up. She chased Sue. Then she ordered Sue to stop.

"Why did you run?" she asked.

"I am due home."

"You can't go!" snarled the wolf. "I want you to play your flute!"

This time Sue blew a new tune. **5**

Stop and Think

5 If you were Sue, how would you feel now?

If I were Sue, I would feel _____

_____

_____

Again the wolf grew tired. She dozed off and started to snore. So Sue ran. She went a few steps. But the wolf woke up. "Little girl! Why did you run?"

"You scare me! And I want to go."

The wolf frowned. "I want you to continue to play!" she commanded.

Sue played her tune. Again, the wolf grew tired. She fell to the ground and slept, snoring loudly. **6**

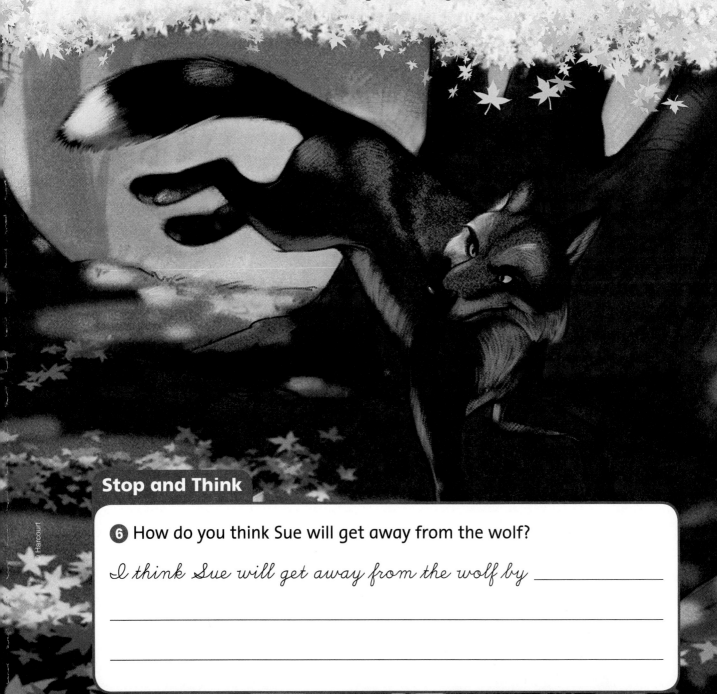

Stop and Think

6 How do you think Sue will get away from the wolf?

I think Sue will get away from the wolf by _____

_____

_____

©Harcourt

Now Sue had a plan. This time she ran a few steps. Then she stopped and blew on her flute. The wolf didn't wake up! Her snoring grew louder! This did the trick! Sue was delighted.

Sue used her cunning new trick a few more times. At last, she was safe at home.

Sue ran to her mom and embraced her. Mom was glad Sue was safe! But she was mad that Sue had broken their rule.

From that time on, Sue stuck to the rules. She never went into the huge forest again! It's true! **7**

Stop and Think

7 What did you learn from this story?

I learned that _____

_____

_____

Think Critically

1. How do things change for Sue during the story? Copy the chart, and fill it in. COMPARE AND CONTRAST

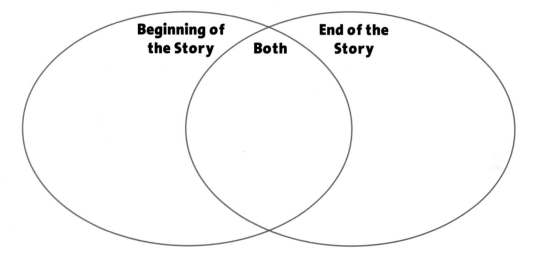

Beginning of the Story   **Both**   **End of the Story**

2. Why does Sue get into trouble with the wolf? CAUSE AND EFFECT

Sue gets into trouble because _____

_____

3. How does Sue get away from the wolf? PLOT

Sue gets away from the wolf when she _____

_____

_____

burden

console

drowsy

glancing

heroic

scolding

Vocabulary

Build Robust Vocabulary

Write the Vocabulary Word that completes each sentence in the newspaper articles. The first one has been done for you.

DAILY NEWS   SECTION C

Big Deer Drinks River

Monday, July 27

A big deer came to the river this morning. It's drinking up all the water. Other animals came to stop the deer. "Shame on you, Deer!" yelled a beaver. But

(1) _____scolding_____ the deer didn't help.

Badger said, "Other animals have tried to

(2) _____ me. But I will not feel better until that deer has been stopped."

© Harcourt

Save the River!

Tuesday, July 28

A big deer is still drinking up the river. The water will

not last much longer. Anyone can see this just by

(3) _____ at the river.

Some hope that a (4) _____

animal will save the river. Others hope the deer will get

(5) _____ and go to sleep. One plan

was to lift the deer. But the big deer is too much of a

(6) _____ to do this. Someone must

think of a way to save the river.

171

How Flea Saved the River

by Wiley Gaby

illustrated by Christine Jenny

CAST OF ANIMALS

EAGLE	BEAVER
DEER	FLEA
BADGER	FISH

SETTING: In a forest long ago.

EAGLE: When I was a little eagle, a big, deep river ran to meet the blue sea. It was filled with clean water. Fish leaped up from its waves. Beavers, badgers, and fish made their homes in the water. Big and small beasts came to drink from it. One hot summer, Deer arrived from the East. He needed water because he had traveled very far. **1**

Stop and Think

1 What do you think Deer will most likely do next?

I think that Deer will _____

_____

_____

DEER: *(Comes in stage right.)*: I'm weak, and I have such thirst. I need a bit of water. *(Deer pretends to drink from the river.)*

EAGLE: That big deer seemed to need more than a bit of water. He drank that water down and didn't stop. The water started to disappear!

BADGER: *(Comes in from trees.)*: Deer needs to stop. I'll have nowhere to sleep! ❷

Stop and Think

❷ Where do you think Badger has his home?

I think Badger's home is _____

_____

_____

© Harcourt

EAGLE: Badger pleaded with Deer to stop. But he was drinking so fast that he didn't hear Badger. The water kept going down.

BADGER: (*Leaping up and down.*) Please, sir! I beg you to stop! This river will turn into a little stream if you keep drinking!

EAGLE: Still, Deer drank. Badger ran for help. (*Badger runs off stage.*)

DEER: Yes! This sweet water is such a treat! ❸

Stop and Think

❸ Why is Badger upset with Deer?

Badger is upset because _____

_____

_____

©Harcourt

EAGLE: Badger came back with Beaver and Flea. They were all the help he could find. *(Badger, Beaver, and Flea run in from the trees. Flea tries to console Badger to make him feel better.)*

FLEA: There, there, Badger. Somehow we will stop Deer.

BADGER: You see? Deer will drink all the water in the river. In no time, it will turn into a little creek! Please stop him!

BEAVER: What can we do?

EAGLE: A fish leaped out of the water to see what was happening. It would be a big problem for the fish if there was no water.

FISH: Please, stop drinking all of the river. We fish will have nowhere to go! *(Fish exits off stage.)* **4**

Stop and Think

4 How is Fish different from the other animals?

This is how Fish is different: _____

_____

_____

EAGLE: Each animal tried to think of how to make Deer stop.

EAGLE: We can lift him up and take him away!

FLEA: That would be too big a burden. Deer is much too big for us to lift.

BADGER: We can offer him green plants to eat!

EAGLE: Beaver tried scolding him.

BEAVER: You are being selfish. Shame on you!

EAGLE: Then little Flea started to speak.

FLEA: I think I can make him stop drinking.

BADGER: Flea, you can't beat a deer!

BEAVER: Why, fleas are smaller than peas!

BADGER: Fleas are no bigger than seeds! **5**

Stop and Think

5 Do you think a flea can stop a deer? Why or why not?

I think a flea _____

_____

_____

176

FLEA: Watch and see! You have to trust me.

EAGLE: Flea hopped to Deer with ease. Then Flea bit hard on Deer's legs.

FLEA: That'll teach you!

EAGLE: Deer stamped his feet and snapped his tail. Deer kept glancing down at his feet, but he didn't see little Flea. So he kept on drinking. Then Flea hopped closer and bit again. Deer stamped his feet harder. Each time he stamped his feet, Deer poked holes in the ground. Water from under the ground filled up the holes. The water ran over and started to fill up the river! **6**

Stop and Think

6 Why does the river start to fill up again?

The river fills up because _____

_____

_____

EAGLE: At last, Deer couldn't take it anymore. He ran into the trees with Flea still nipping at his heels. Deer left to seek out another spot to get a drink. So you see, that heroic flea saved the river!

BEAVER: Flea is smaller than a bean.

BADGER: But she still defeated that big deer!

(Flea enters, tired.)

EAGLE: Flea was drowsy. It had been hard work to save the river. So Flea went to sleep. And by the time she woke up the next morning, the river was filled up again. **7**

Stop and Think

7 How would you feel if you were Flea?

If I were Flea, I would feel _____

_____

_____

Think Critically

1. How are Flea and Deer the same? How are they different? Copy the chart, and fill it in. **COMPARE AND CONTRAST**

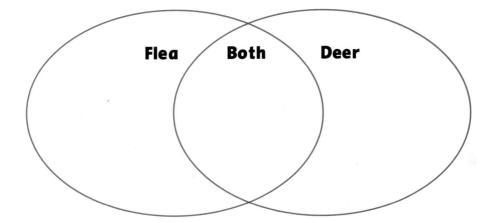

Flea   Both   Deer

2. What do you learn from this story? **AUTHOR'S PURPOSE**

I learn that _____

_____

_____

3. How is the animals' problem solved? **CONFLICT/RESOLUTION**

The animals' problem is solved when _____

_____

_____

_____

crept

glorious

memory

ruined

streak

yanked

Vocabulary

Build Robust Vocabulary

Write the Vocabulary Word that completes each sentence in the postcards. The first one has been done for you.

Dear Dad,

It's not so bad on Gramps' farm. I no longer feel that my summer is **(1)** _____ruined_____. I saw two blue jays **(2)** _____ by Gramps' truck. They were going fast.

Missing you,

Kay

Dad

1211 Main Street

Evanston, IL 60202

Think Critically

1. How are Flea and Deer the same? How are they different? Copy the chart, and fill it in. **COMPARE AND CONTRAST**

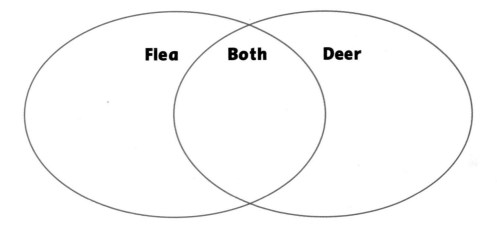

Flea   **Both**   **Deer**

2. What do you learn from this story? **AUTHOR'S PURPOSE**

*I learn that*_____

_____

_____

3. How is the animals' problem solved? **CONFLICT/RESOLUTION**

The animals' problem is solved when _____

_____

_____

© Harcourt

crept

glorious

memory

ruined

streak

yanked

Vocabulary

Build Robust Vocabulary

Write the Vocabulary Word that completes each sentence in the postcards. The first one has been done for you.

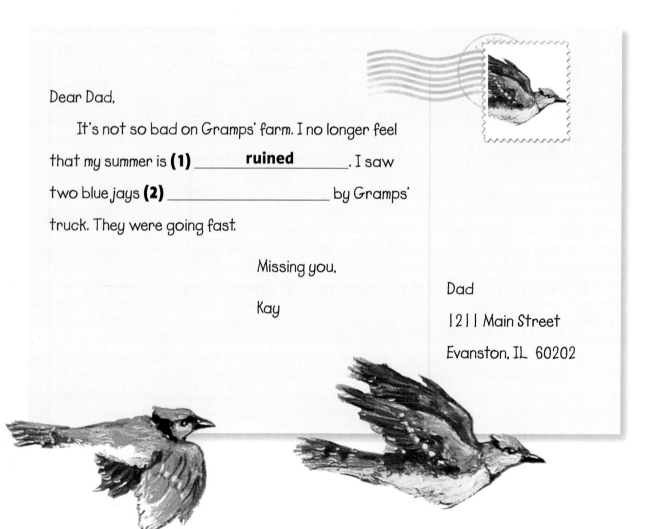

Dear Dad,

It's not so bad on Gramps' farm. I no longer feel that my summer is **(1)** _____**ruined**_____. I saw two blue jays **(2)** _____ by Gramps' truck. They were going fast.

Missing you,

Kay

Dad

1211 Main Street

Evanston, IL 60202

180

© Harcourt

Dear April,

　　I had a **(3)** _____ day with Gramps. It was terrific! We went fishing. I'm still afraid of the cows. When we went to the pond, I slowly **(4)** _____ past them. I didn't want them to see me.

　　　　　　　　　Having fun,

　　　　　　　　　Kay

April Brown

323 Fourth Street

Evanston, IL 60202

Dear Dad,

　　I got a fish! I felt something tug on my line. Then I **(5)** _____ on the rod and reeled in a big fish. I'll never forget it! It will be my best **(6)** _____ of Gramps' farm.

　　　　　　　　　Hugs,

　　　　　　　　　Kay

Dad

1211 Main Street

Evanston, IL 60202

Gramps and the Fiddle Barn

by Wiley Gaby

illustrated by Joel Spector

Kay lived in a big town with her dad. Her home was on Main Street. There was always a lot to do in her town. She painted. She played her flute. She went with her dad to see plays. Kay never wanted to go away from her town.

One May, Kay got a letter. It was from Gramps. Gramps had a farm far away. Summer was near, and Gramps wanted her to come visit. Kay had never been away from home before. **1**

Stop and Think

1 What does Kay like to do in her town? Underline the words that tell you.

Kay likes to _____

_____

Kay's dad had lived on the farm when he was a kid. "You'll have fun, Kay!" he claimed.

"I want to stay here," Kay cried. "Summer will be ruined if I leave!"

"Gramps will take you to the fair. He will take you for hikes on the trails. And in the barn, you can play in the hay. Wait and see."

"No way," said Kay. "This is not fair."

But in a few days, Kay and her dad were on a train. **2**

Stop and Think

2 Why do you think Kay wants to stay home?

I think Kay wants to stay home because _____

_____

_____

The train traveled for a long time! Kay drew pictures of the towns that they passed. She played games with her dad. She played with her doll and braided its hair. Kay had a long wait.

At last, the train stopped. Rain was falling when she stepped off the train. Things seemed so gray. Then Kay spotted a man with a wave of gray in his hair. Gramps!

"Let's get out of this rain, Kay," Gramps said. They both waved good-bye to her dad. Then Gramps grabbed her suitcase, and they walked to his truck. ❸

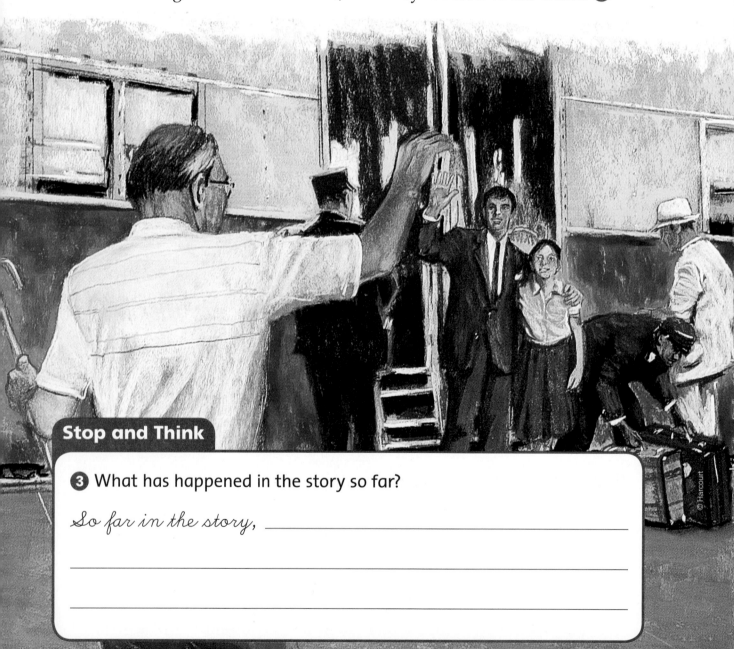

Stop and Think

❸ What has happened in the story so far?

So far in the story, _____

_____

_____

Gramps didn't say much as he drove to the farm. Kay stared out at the land. She missed Main Street and her dad.

The rain stopped. Rays of sunshine peeked out from the clouds. Kay watched a pair of blue jays streak by. She sniffed the fresh air. Maybe a few days with Gramps would not be too bad. **4**

Stop and Think

4 What do you think will happen next?

I think that _____

_____

_____

185

Gramps had a plain farmhouse. He grew grain and hay, and he raised cows. Kay was afraid of those cows. They were big and had long tails. She was glad the cows stayed in the barn.

Each day, Gramps did things with Kay. They went to the fair. They hiked. Kay's dad was right! She didn't paint or see plays. But it was fun anyway!

Gramps was fun, too. They hunted for snails. Gramps and Kay went fishing, and they used the snails for bait. After a few days with Gramps, Kay wanted to stay. **5**

Stop and Think

5 How does Kay feel about staying with Gramps now? Underline the words that tell you.

Now Kay feels _____

_____

186

One Sunday, Gramps went to his barn. He stayed there all day. Kay played inside the house. She sent letters to her dad. And she grew bored. Kay wanted to see what Gramps was up to.

When Kay got to the barn, she didn't hear just cows. She could hear wonderful notes made by instruments! The air was filled with these glorious sounds. She strained to sneak a peek into the window, but she was too short. She grabbed a pail and turned it upside down. She crept up on it and peered inside. Kay could see Gramps. **6**

Stop and Think

6 Why does Kay look in the barn?

Kay looks in the barn because _____

_____

_____

Gramps was playing a fiddle! Some other men were playing instruments, too.

Kay jumped down, yanked up her pail, and ran inside.

"Pull up your pail, Kay," said Gramps.

Kay clapped and played her pail like a drum. "Yes!" Kay shouted. "This is the best summer ever!"

On that day, Kay named the barn the Fiddle Barn. After that, she paid Gramps and his barn a visit each year. Sometimes her dad came, too. From then on, summers on Main Street were just a distant memory. **7**

Stop and Think

7 What does the author want you to understand from this story?

The author wants me to understand that _____

_____

_____

188

Think Critically

1. Think about the story and how it ends. Copy the chart, and fill it in. **PLOT**

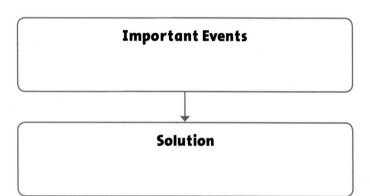

Important Events

↓

Solution

2. What happens to change Kay's mind about visiting Gramps? **CAUSE AND EFFECT**

Kay changes her mind about visiting Gramps when _____

_____

3. Did the author write this story to entertain you or to inform you? Explain your answer. **AUTHOR'S PURPOSE**

The author wrote this story _____

_____

_____

enormous

exclaimed

overheard

suggested

swift

vain

Vocabulary

Build Robust Vocabulary

Read the story and think about the meanings of the words in dark type.

One egg was still to hatch. Hen didn't know what to do. Goat **overheard** the news. He **suggested** the egg was bad. But, at last, a little chick popped out! But this chick was different. He had one wing and one leg.

With just one leg, the little chick was not very **swift.** But everyone liked him. He began to think he was better than the rest. The little chick became a bit **vain.** He felt so important that he went to see the king. When he reached the king's **enormous** house, there were two men who kept watch at the gate. "The king *will* want to see you," one of the men **exclaimed.**

© Harcourt

Write the Vocabulary Word that completes each sentence. The first one has been done for you.

1. With just one leg, the chick was not fast.

He was not _____ **swift** _____ .

2. The king's home is very big. It's

_____ .

3. Goat _____

that one egg had not hatched.

4. Goat thought the egg was bad.

He _____ this to hen.

5. The little chick acted a bit _____ .

He felt that he was better than the rest.

6. One man _____ ,"The king *will* want

to see you."

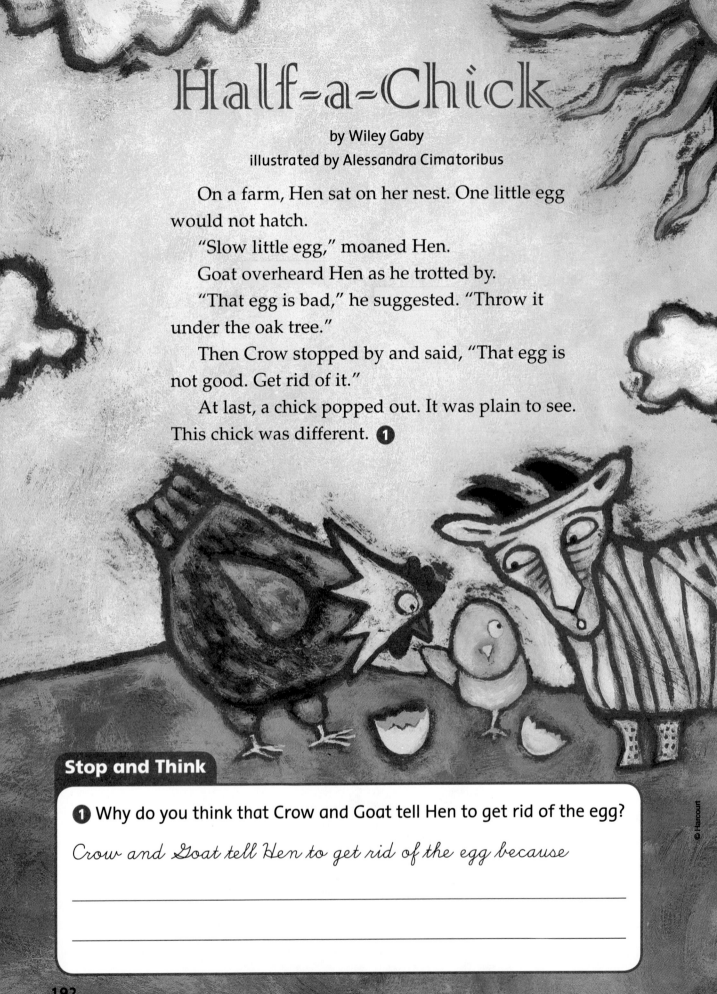

Half-a-Chick

by Wiley Gaby

illustrated by Alessandra Cimatoribus

On a farm, Hen sat on her nest. One little egg would not hatch.

"Slow little egg," moaned Hen.

Goat overheard Hen as he trotted by.

"That egg is bad," he suggested. "Throw it under the oak tree."

Then Crow stopped by and said, "That egg is not good. Get rid of it."

At last, a chick popped out. It was plain to see. This chick was different. ❶

Stop and Think

❶ Why do you think that Crow and Goat tell Hen to get rid of the egg?

Crow and Goat tell Hen to get rid of the egg because

_____

_____

"Whoa," Goat said. "Your chick has one leg and one wing." He was just one half of a chick. He became known as Half-a-Chick.

"Half-a-Chick is the best," Hen liked to boast. "He'll be known from coast to coast."

Half-a-Chick grew up. He got to know everyone. Everyone liked him. But he grew a bit vain. He began to think he had better things to do.

"This little farm has grown too small for me. I know the king is down the road. I bet the king would want to see *me*."

So he left. ❷

Stop and Think

❷ How is the new chick special?

The new chick is special because _____

_____

_____

193

On the road, Half-a-Chick found a stream blocked by a fallen oak tree. The stream called out, "Help me, please! This tree is stuck. Boats can't float by."

Half-a-Chick cleared the tree out of the way. Then he went on down the road. He had no time to play.

Next, Half-a-Chick came across a small fire. Its flame burned low. "Help me, please," the fire said. "My coals are weak. Fan me with your wing."  ❸

Stop and Think

❸ How do you know that Half-a-Chick will help the fire?

I know Half-a-Chick will help the fire because _____

_____

_____

Half-a-Chick fanned the coals. The flames grew bigger and stronger. Those coals did not need his help any longer. Half-a-Chick hopped on. His goal was to visit the king down the road.

Before long, he came upon the wind tangled in sticks. The wind begged, "Can I ask for your help? Please, Half-a-Chick?"

Half-a-Chick helped the wind and went on his way. There was no more time for stopping. There was no time for play. ❹

Stop and Think

❹ Who is in this story? Where does the story take place?

The characters are _____

The story takes place_____

_____

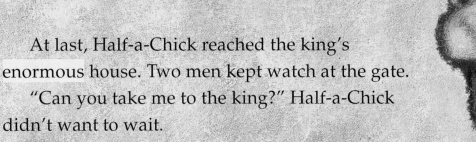

At last, Half-a-Chick reached the king's enormous house. Two men kept watch at the gate.

"Can you take me to the king?" Half-a-Chick didn't want to wait.

The men stared. "Just who are you?" they asked.

"I'm Half-a-Chick. The king will want to see me!"

"Yes, the king *will* want to see you . . . in his kitchen!" exclaimed one of the men. He picked up Half-a-Chick and tossed him into a pot of water. **5**

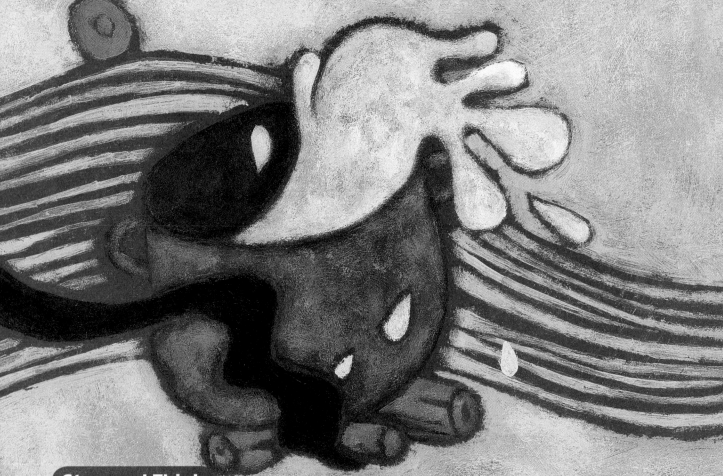

Stop and Think

5 How do you think Half-a-Chick feels after the man throws him into a pot of water? Why?

I think Half-a-Chick feels _____

_____

© Harcourt

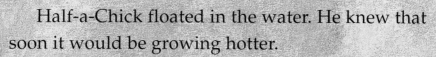

Half-a-Chick floated in the water. He knew that soon it would be growing hotter.

"This is no way to visit the king!" he cried. Half-a-Chick was afraid he was on his own. Then he remembered his new friends.

"Fire! Help me!" he cried. "Please don't burn me."

The fire said, "You helped me. Now I'll help you. Ask the water to put me out."

The water was happy to help. It splashed out of the pot and put out the fire. ❻

Stop and Think

❻ Why do the fire and the water help Half-a-Chick?

The fire and the water help Half-a-Chick because

_____

_____

The swift wind was next to help. It lifted Half-a-Chick out of the pot and out a window. Then it set Half-a-Chick on top of the king's house.

Now we *do* know Half-a-Chick from coast to coast. He became the first wind vane. To this day, you can find Half-a-Chick up on house tops, showing us which way the wind blows. **7**

Stop and Think

7 Why is it important to help others?

It is important to help others because _____

_____

_____

Think Critically

1. What problem did Half-a-Chick have once he arrived at the king's home? How was the problem solved? Copy the chart, and fill it in. PROBLEM/SOLUTION

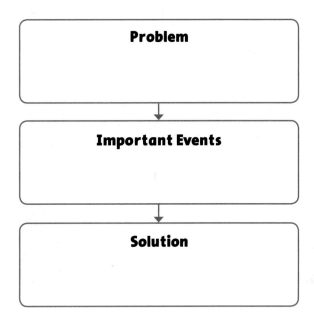

Problem

↓

Important Events

↓

Solution

2. What does the author want you to learn from this story? AUTHOR'S PURPOSE

The author wants me to learn _____

_____

3. What happens to Half-a-Chick at the end of the story? Were his mother's predictions right? PLOT

At the end of the story, Half-a-Chick _____

_____

_____

Vocabulary

Build Robust Vocabulary

Write the word that best completes each sentence. The first one has been done for you.

1. The conductor can tell us more about the Gold Coast Band. Let's have a _____**dialogue**_____ with him.

   dialogue   rehearse   memory

2. To play songs well, the band must _____ many times.

   criticize   rehearse   immerse

3. It's _____ for the lead

   swift   mandatory   enormous

   singer to sing her part over and over. She must get the notes right.

4. The band likes to play new

_____ of older songs.

dialogues   streaks   versions

5. The band members train for weeks. They

_____ themselves in

immerse   criticize   burden

the songs. They will know them well.

6. The conductor always says kind things

to the children. He does not like to

_____ the way they sing or play.

immerse   criticize   console

Write the answers to these questions.
Use complete sentences.

7. Why is it mandatory to rehearse the songs?

_____

_____

8. Does the conductor criticize the children? Explain.

_____

_____

Finding Facts at the Theater

by Wiley Gaby

illustrated by Mike Tofanelli

Cast Of Characters

Faith	Ben	Conductor
Soloist	Violinist	Chorus

Faith: We are reporting from behind the curtain at the Gold Coast Theater.

Ben: The Gold Coast Band will play both old and new songs this evening.

Faith: We have some band members with us.

Ben: Let's have a dialogue with the conductor. He can tell us what it takes to put on a show.

Chorus: Let's begin! ❶

Stop and Think

❶ What do you think it takes to put on a show?

To put on a show, I think it takes _____

_____

_____

© Harcourt

Conductor: Hello! I am glad you are here.

Ben: Thank you for letting us talk to you before the show. We would like to find out what your job is as a conductor.

Conductor: First, I find the tunes for the band to play. Next, I find those students that best play each instrument. Then, I find students that sing well. After that, we begin to prepare for a show.

Chorus: There must be lots to do. ②

Stop and Think

② What does the conductor do after finding tunes to play?

After finding tunes to play, the conductor _____

_____

_____

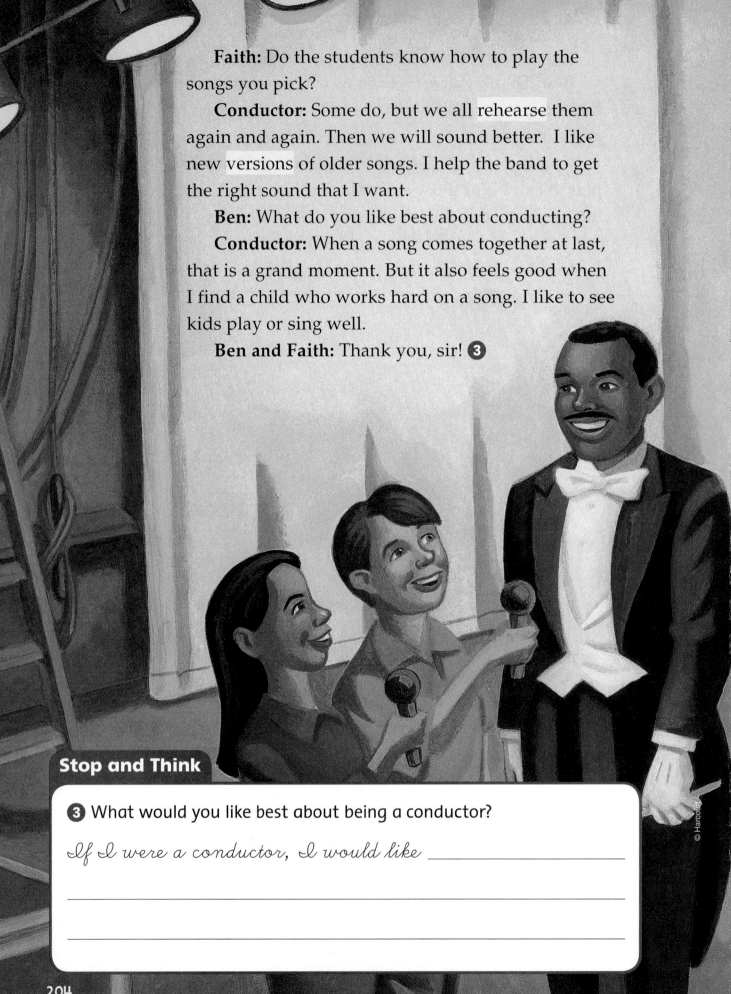

Faith: Do the students know how to play the songs you pick?

Conductor: Some do, but we all rehearse them again and again. Then we will sound better. I like new versions of older songs. I help the band to get the right sound that I want.

Ben: What do you like best about conducting?

Conductor: When a song comes together at last, that is a grand moment. But it also feels good when I find a child who works hard on a song. I like to see kids play or sing well.

Ben and Faith: Thank you, sir! ❸

Stop and Think

❸ What would you like best about being a conductor?

If I were a conductor, I would like _____

_____

_____

Ben: Here is one of the singers. Are you a soloist?

Chorus: A soloist sings or plays alone.

Soloist: Yes. I have a part that I sing by myself.

Faith: So tell us what it's like to sing alone.

Soloist: I like it now. But I was scared when the conductor told me that I had a solo.

Chorus: I think most of us would be scared!

Soloist: But then I was pleased! It's an important part. Because I sing alone, it was mandatory for me to rehearse my part. I wanted to sing correctly, *and* be in time with the band. ❹

Stop and Think

❹ What is a soloist? Underline the words that tell you.

A soloist is someone who _____

_____

_____

© Harcourt

Ben: What did you discover with all that work?

Soloist: I could hold notes better and longer. I discovered how to use my lungs to make my tones strong. I think it has paid off.

Faith: Are all chorus members soloists?

Chorus: No, but we all have to train for weeks. We immerse ourselves in the songs for a long time! That way we know them very well.

Faith: Was that work or fun?

Chorus: Both, but we didn't mind! **5**

Stop and Think

5 What do the soloist and the chorus say about all the hard work?

The soloist and chorus both say _____

_____

_____

206

© Harcourt

Ben: I would like to ask the conductor, is it hard to teach children to sing and play?

Conductor: Each child in this band is first-rate! It is hard to criticize the way children sing or play. I want to say things that will help them do their best.

Faith: What was the hardest thing about putting together a show like this?

Conductor: I needed to find children who play instruments. We needed a child who plays the violin.

Ben: Did you find one?

Conductor: I found a violin player who was in third grade. He is better than most. Here he is! **6**

Stop and Think

6 Why did the conductor choose a violinist in the third grade?

The conductor chose a violinist in the third grade because

_____

_____

Violinist: Both my mom and dad play violin. I have played most of my life.

Ben: How do you prepare for the show?

Violinist: We put on our best clothes. We relax so we are not shaking when we start.

Faith: And this show is about to start!

Conductor: Yes, it is! We must go!

Ben: Thanks to all of you. Have a good show.

Faith: I think it's time to take our seats.

Ben: Let's go! **7**

Stop and Think

7 How are the soloist and the violinist different?

The soloist and the violinist are different because _____

_____

_____

Think Critically

1. How do you think the band members feel as the show is starting? **CHARACTERS**

   As the show is starting, I think the band

   members feel _____

   _____

2. What are some of the things that go into a good performance? **DRAW CONCLUSIONS**

   These are some of the things that go into a good

   performance: _____

   _____

3. What is the main idea of this play? **MAIN IDEA AND DETAILS**

   The main idea of this play is _____

   _____

   _____

Vocabulary

Build Robust Vocabulary

Write the Vocabulary Word that completes each sentence. The first one has been done for you.

In Antarctica, there is always a frozen sheet of ice. It

(1) _____**permanently**_____ blankets the land. Antarctica is really

a frozen desert.

In winter, there is an **(2)** _____ of light.

It's dark all the time. The **(3)** _____ light gives

little heat. Few animals stay on the land during the winter.

When spring comes, the sea is rich with plants

that **(4)** _____ in the water.

More animals come to eat the plants.

Snow petrels are small, white birds. They come to Antarctica when summer begins. They look for **(5)** _____ from the cold. They make their nests in safe spots. Leaves and grass are **(6)** _____ , so they line their nests with pebbles.

Write the answers to these questions.
Use complete sentences.

7. Why do snow petrels look for shelter?

_____

_____

8. Why do you think leaves and grass are scarce in Antarctica? _____

_____

_____

SNOW BIRDS

by Nancy Furstinger

Antarctica is the world's coldest spot. It can be 100 degrees below zero. Little rain or snow falls here. The air and land are dry. A frozen sheet of ice permanently blankets the land. Antarctica is really a frozen desert.

In Antarctica, June is the start of winter. In winter, there is an absence of light in the sky. The days are very short. It is dark all of the time! ❶

Stop and Think

❶ What do you know about Antarctica so far?

Antarctica is _____
_____
_____

In winter, the **dim** light of the sun gives little heat. Few animals stay on the land during this time. The biggest of these is an insect. It is a kind of fly without wings!

Then spring comes in September. Days get longer. The sun's rays shine into the sea. The sea is rich with small plants. These plants soak up the sun's rays as they **drift** in the water. Little animals called krill swim by and eat the plants. Bigger fish feed on the plants and krill. All three are food for seals, whales, and birds. ②

Stop and Think

② Why is it difficult for animals to live on Antarctica's land in the winter?

It is difficult because _____

_____

As spring arrives, so do more animals. Many kinds of seals swim in the cold water by the shore. They eat the krill and fish. They will have their babies on the nearby land.

Birds also make their homes here. Some birds cannot fly, but they are good swimmers. They waddle and slide across the snow. They will hatch their eggs on land.

Summer arrives in December and so do whales. They come to feed on the krill. Later, they will go to northern waters to have their babies. But for now, this is a good spot to find food. **3**

Stop and Think

3 How do some birds use the snow to move?

Some birds use the snow to _____

_____

_____

Many flying birds appear when summer starts, and the sea is full of fish. They will fly to the nearby shore to make their nests.

Some of these birds are petrels. Petrels are like sea gulls. Their strong wings let them fly far from land. Their thick coats and webbed feet help them live in the cold. Most birds do not have a sense of smell. But not these! They can sniff out a meal. **4**

Stop and Think

4 What do petrels have that helps them live in Antarctica?

To help them live in Antarctica, petrels have _____

_____

_____

Snow petrels are much smaller than other petrels. They are about the size of a robin. Their coats are as white as snow. They match the land around them! Just their black bills, eyes, and feet stand out against all of that white. When they fly, they flutter like bats! **5**

Stop and Think

5 What do you learn about snow petrels?

I learn that snow petrels _____

_____

_____

Snow petrels are shy. If bothered, they may just fly away. But if something gets too close, they have a sly trick. They can spit out a liquid that smells very bad!

These birds fly low over the sea when they want to find food. They spy their dinner from above and dart into the water to catch it. After they eat, they roll in the snow to clean sea salt off their coats. **6**

Stop and Think

6 What do petrels do after they catch and eat their meals?

After they catch and eat their meals, petrels _____

_____

_____

Once a snow petrel finds a partner, the pair will make a nest. A safe spot shelters the nest from other animals. Leaves and grass are scarce. So they line their nests with small pebbles.

The female lays just one white egg. About six weeks later, the chick hatches. It grows fast. In seven weeks it will be ready to fly away. By staying safe, it may fly for up to twenty years in the Antarctic sky. **7**

Stop and Think

7 Why do petrels line their nests with pebbles?

They line their nests with pebbles because _____

_____

_____

Think Critically

1. What steps does a petrel take to make a nest and lay eggs? Copy the chart, fill it in. SEQUENCE

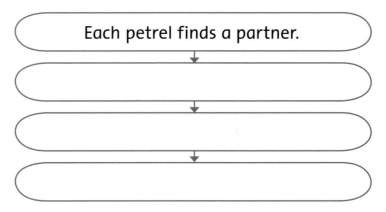

Each petrel finds a partner.

2. How are the seals and the birds of Antarctica alike? How are they different? COMPARE AND CONTRAST

*Here are the ways they are alike:*_____

_____

_____

*Here are the ways they are different:*_____

_____

_____

3. Why don't snow petrels live in Antarctica during winter?
MAIN IDEA AND DETAILS

They don't live in Antarctica during winter

*because*_____

_____

detail
dozes
effort
fluttering
nocturnal
swoops

Vocabulary

Build Robust Vocabulary

Write the Vocabulary Word that completes each sentence in the postcards. The first one has been done for you.

Dear Mark,

Owl watching is fun! This postcard shows an owl as it **(1)** _____ swoops _____ out of a tree to catch a meal. We have to stay awake at night to see the owls. They are

(2) _____ animals.

Your friend,

Steve

Mark Steel

1456 Fair Ave.

Broomall, PA 19008

Dear Mark,

Last night, an owl tried to catch a skunk.

We saw its wings

(3) _____

as it flew past us. The owl made a good

(4) _____ , but it missed.

No skunk for that owl! I wish you could be here with

us. You would have so much fun!

Your friend in the wild,

Steve

Mark Steel

1456 Fair Ave.

Broomall, PA 19008

Dear Mark,

I stayed up too late last night. I need rest

before my next adventure. Dad gets tired, too.

He **(5)** _____ off in the

middle of the day.

There's more fun stuff to tell you about. I'll share

every **(6)** _____ of my trip

when I get home.

See you soon,

Steve

Mark Steel

1456 Fair Ave.

Broomall, PA 19008

Flying Tigers

by Nancy Furstinger
illustrated by Patrick Gnan

The night is bright. "Who's awake?" a horned owl calls. "I am!" he seems to say.

The horned owl stirs from his perch high in a tree. This mighty bird stretches his wings. He's ready to take a night flight. This owl is nocturnal. He sleeps during the day and is awake at twilight. His eyes and ears will help him hunt tonight. **1**

Stop and Think

1 When does a nocturnal bird sleep? When is the bird awake?

A nocturnal bird sleeps _____

It is awake _____

_____

The horned owl hears more owls reply to his call. He swoops from the height of his perch. His flight is silent. He looks like a flying tiger.

His wings span up to 60 inches. The soft, brown plumes have black tips. These colors help him blend with the trees at daylight. His plumes form little peaks that look like ears or horns.

A horned owl has bright yellow eyes. He always looks forward. When he turns his neck, the owl can see to the side. He tilts his neck to locate sounds. He can hear a mouse running under 12 inches of snow! **2**

Stop and Think

2 To what does the author compare the horned owl?

The author compares the horned owl to _____

_____

_____

The horned owl glides in a slow spin. His sharp eyes and ears spot a skunk. The flying tiger folds his mighty wings. He opens his strong talons and dives to the ground. The owl is as fast as lightning.

The owl gives the skunk quite a fright. The skunk sticks his tail upright. He fires a spray that stinks. Then the skunk runs into the night.  **3**

Stop and Think

3 What does the skunk do after the owl frightens him?

After the owl frightens him, the skunk _____

_____

_____

The horned owl made an effort to catch the skunk. Now he smells of skunk, but he can't tell. An owl can't smell very well.

Now the owl wades into water. He sees a fish fluttering his tail. He grabs the fish tight. He gulps it down in one bite.

Long after his meal, the owl will spit out a pellet. This holds the fish's bones. Pellets can hold fur, teeth, and quills. These details show what the owl ate.

Again, the owl sees a fish. His mighty talons grab again. But he will not eat this second fish. He catches this fish for another owl. **4**

Stop and Think

4 How can you tell what an owl ate for dinner?

I can tell what an owl ate for dinner by _____

_____

_____

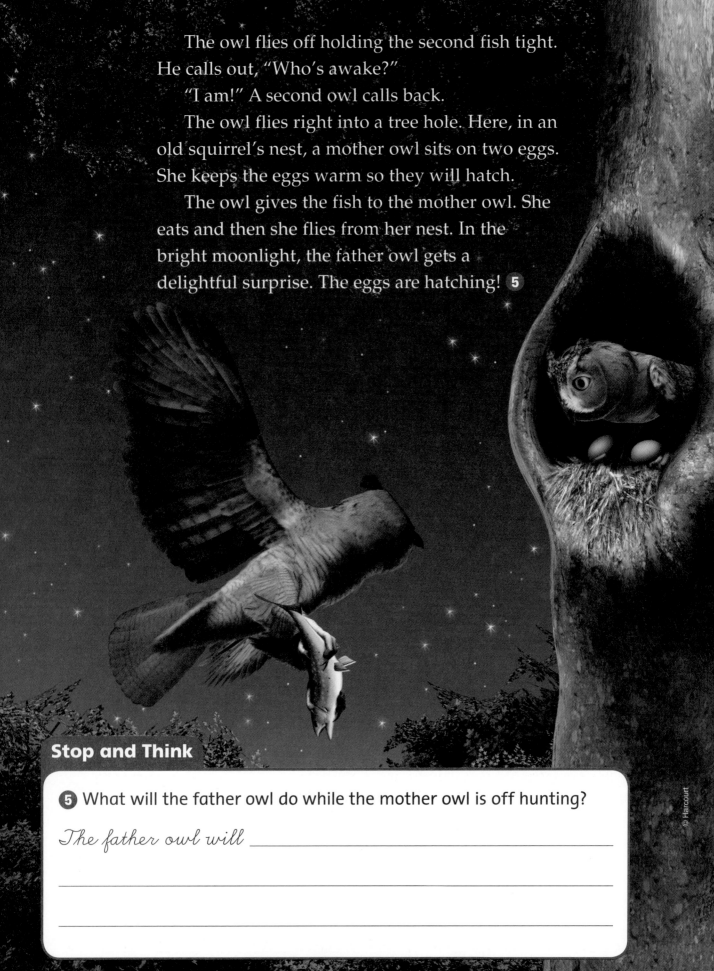

The owl flies off holding the second fish tight. He calls out, "Who's awake?"

"I am!" A second owl calls back.

The owl flies right into a tree hole. Here, in an old squirrel's nest, a mother owl sits on two eggs. She keeps the eggs warm so they will hatch.

The owl gives the fish to the mother owl. She eats and then she flies from her nest. In the bright moonlight, the father owl gets a delightful surprise. The eggs are hatching! **5**

Stop and Think

5 What will the father owl do while the mother owl is off hunting?

The father owl will _____

_____

_____

Daylight draws near. The pair sees a fox on the prowl. It strays too close. The father owl puts up a fight. The frightened fox runs off.

The owls both doze. Under their warm bodies, the white eggs hatch. Two owls are born at the first light of morning. They screech with hunger. It sounds like steam blasting through pipes! Now the mother and father owl take turns. They must hunt for food day and night. **6**

Stop and Think

6 What happens after the owls see a fox?

After the owls see a fox, _____

_____

_____

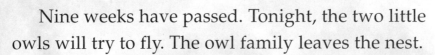

Nine weeks have passed. Tonight, the two little owls will try to fly. The owl family leaves the nest.

The little owls take just a short flight. They fly to a second perch. There, they hold on tight.

Each time they fly, the two owls will go a little higher and a little farther. In the fall, they will disappear from sight. And they will call, "Who's awake? I am!" **7**

Stop and Think

7 When will it be time for the baby owls to leave the nest?

It will be time for the baby owls to leave the nest when

_____

_____

Think Critically

1. Why would a nocturnal owl need to hunt during the day?
DRAW CONCLUSIONS

A nocturnal owl would hunt during the day

_____

_____

2. What do the owls do to catch a fish? Copy the chart, and fill
it in. **SEQUENCE**

> Owl wades into water.

↓

>

↓

>

↓

>

3. What details show you that owls are good parents? **MAIN
IDEA AND DETAILS**

These details show me that owls are good parents:

_____

_____

decent

disgraceful

emotion

fondness

inherit

ridiculous

Vocabulary

Build Robust Vocabulary

Read the story and think about the meanings of the words in dark type.

The villagers of Orange Grove were **decent** folks. They always smiled and greeted each other with a happy **emotion.** They also had a strong **fondness** for oranges. Orange trees grew everywhere.

One day, the queen of the land challenged the residents to grow the biggest orange. The winner would **inherit** all her riches. It was a **ridiculous** contest. Everyone changed. The villagers acted **disgraceful.** They didn't smile or help each other anymore.

© Harcourt

Write the Vocabulary Word that completes each sentence. The first one has been done for you.

1. The villagers liked oranges. They had a

   _____**fondness**_____ for them.

2. Before the contest, the villagers greeted each other

   with a happy _____ .

3. The winner of the challenge would be rich. They would

   _____ the queen's riches.

4. The contest was very silly. It was

   _____ .

5. The villagers did not act right. The way they acted was

   _____ .

6. The villagers used to be good. They were

   _____ folks before the contest.

The Ridiculous Challenge

by Nancy Furstinger
illustrated by Robert Byrd

Say hello to the town of Orange Grove. It's a gentle village at the top of a ridge. The villagers here are a decent bunch. Each day they greet each other. They smile as they pass, and are helpful in general. These residents of Orange Grove have the same strange habit. They all have a strong fondness for oranges.

Orange trees are everywhere. There are orange trees near bridges and next to the gym. There are orange trees near sidewalks and next to the roads. These villagers like their oranges. In fact, each cottage has a prized orange tree in the yard. ❶

Stop and Think

❶ What do the villagers do that shows they are a decent bunch?

The villagers show they are a decent bunch when

Villagers of all ages use the oranges in many ways. Mrs. Page gives away huge glasses of orange drink. Miss Spot trains her dog Angel and other village pets. She uses small bits of oranges. Mr. George makes an orange fudge that tastes grand. The villagers are glad to share what they grow. And they share the same motto, "We stick our necks out for each other." ❷

Stop and Think

❷ How do the villagers use oranges?

The villagers use oranges to _____

_____

_____

Then one day a beautiful boat sailed under the bridge. The villagers rushed to the dock. They nudged each other as a stranger hopped off. This messenger must be from the queen. They could tell from the badge and the gems on his chest. The villagers bowed their long necks in respect.

"My dear villagers, the queen is having a contest!" declared the messenger. "She challenges all to see which villager can grow the largest orange. The winner will inherit her riches. Three months from today, I will return to judge the oranges. Let the contest begin!" ③

Stop and Think

③ How is the messenger different from the villagers?

Here is how he is different: _____

_____

_____

At first, the villagers chuckled about the contest. But before long, they started to dream. They dreamed about what they could get if they were rich. Miss Spot imagined a beautiful collar for Angel. Mr. George imagined a sports car with a fast engine. Mrs. Page imagined a huge house. Then all began to hide their oranges. They began to plan how they could win the contest. **4**

Stop and Think

4 What do you think will happen next?

I think _____

_____

_____

The tone of the village changed. The villagers spent all of their time with their necks in the trees. Miss Spot put a giant cage around her own tree. Some protected their oranges day and night. Mr. George told everyone to stay away. Mrs. Page set up alarms around her yard. The way everyone was acting was disgraceful. No one was sticking their necks out for each other anymore. ⑤

DANGER
KEEP AWAY

Stop and Think

⑤ Why did the tone of the village change?

The tone of the village changed because _____

_____

_____

Then one day someone let out a fearful cry.

"Help! It's my Angel! He just fell over the edge of the cliff!" cried Miss Spot, full of emotion. The villagers ran to help.

As one, the villagers helped Mr. George reach down over the edge. He grabbed the little dog by the back of the neck. Angel was saved!

Miss Spot said, "Imagine! We could have lost my Angel!" The villagers nodded. All were quiet. **6**

Stop and Think

6 How does Angel bring the villagers together?

Angel brings the villagers together when _____

_____

_____

Mr. George cried, "This challenge is ridiculous! It's a better prize to be friends!"

Then the villagers stuck their necks into their trees. They picked all the oranges and planned a grand feast. They were having such a good time that they didn't hear the messenger arrive.

"Where is the prize orange?" he cried. "Where is *any* orange? No one wins the challenge! There is no winner here." And he left in a huff.

But the villagers were happy. They felt that they were winners already. **7**

Stop and Think

7 How do you think the author feels about friendship?

I think the author feels that _____

_____

_____

238

Think Critically

1. What happens when there are no oranges left to win the contest? Copy the chart, and fill it in. CAUSE AND EFFECT

Cause		Effect
There are no oranges left to win the contest.	→	

2. No one wins the contest. Why do the villagers feel that they are winners in the end? MAKE INFERENCES

The villagers feel that they are winners because

_____

_____

3. Why is the villagers' motto important to the story? PLOT

The villagers' motto is important because

_____

_____

beckoned

clutter

flustered

mentioned

remark

visible

Vocabulary

Build Robust Vocabulary

Write the Vocabulary Word that completes each sentence in the diary. The first one has been done for you.

Sunday

There was stuff all over my bed. I had hoped that Dad wouldn't say anything about the mess. But it was the first thing he **(1)** ___mentioned___ . That's what parents do! "But Dad, I have to think of something to take to show-and-tell," I begged.

"Where's your thinking cap?" he asked. "Can you see it? Is it **(2)** _____ in all this mess?" He winked and I laughed.

Dad is right. I need to pick up all this

(3) _____ .

I had a hard time finding my thinking cap. I got so

(4) _____ that I almost forgot why I

was looking for it. Dad was right to make that

(5) _____ about my mess.

In the end, I did find my thinking cap. It helped! Now I

know what I'm going to take to show-and-tell. I'm going to

take Tattle Tail to class! "Come here, Tattle Tail," I

(6) _____ to my bunny. "We're going to

make the whole class laugh."

Carly's Show and Tell

by Nancy Furstinger

illustrated by John Bendall-Brunello

Carly put on her hat, the one her family called "Carly's Thinking Cap." It was a silly hat, a clutter of colored flowers.

"Is the hat helping?" her father asked.

Carly nodded. Her thinking cap helped every time. Now Carly knew what she would take to show-and-tell.

She grabbed her note cards. Carly printed slowly. She didn't want to miss one idea. Next, Carly called her best friend, Pat. She read her plan off the cards, trying not to laugh too loudly. **1**

Stop and Think

1 What does Carly do when she needs an idea?

When Carly needs an idea, she _____

_____

_____

The next day, Carly boarded the bus. She waited for The Joker to make a remark about the travel bag she carried. He gave her bag a sneaky look, but dodged her frown.

Before class began, Carly slid the travel bag under her desk. "What a relief!" Carly said. "No one on the bus mentioned the bag."

Carly gazed out the window until Mrs. Fox clapped her hands. "It's time for show-and-tell. Who wants to go first?" ❷

Stop and Think

❷ What is the first thing Carly does before class begins?

The first thing Carly does is _____

_____

_____

A sea of hands waved in the air. Kim showed off shells. Mike brought the bike he got for his birthday. Pat held up a kite in the shape of a frog.

Mrs. Fox beckoned. "Carly, I believe you're next."

Carly carried her travel bag up to Mrs. Fox's desk. "I brought Tattle Tail. He is going to be a TV star. Today, Tattle Tail will do tricks."

Carly lifted the flap of her travel bag. Two huge ears became visible. The entire class shrieked in surprise. **3**

Stop and Think

3 What do you think Carly has hidden in her travel bag?

I think Carly has _____

_____

_____

Then a twitchy nose popped out. Tattle Tail jumped onto the floor. He thumped his hind feet.

"What a jolly bunny!" Mrs. Fox said. "Show us what Tattle Tail can do."

"He will hop for treats," Pat yelled.

Carly grabbed a box of treats from her bag. She held one above Tattle Tail. The rabbit rose to his hind legs and hopped. Next, he ran around Carly's chair. Tattle Tail ended his trick by jumping into Carly's lap. **4**

Stop and Think

4 What does Tattle Tail do for Carly's class?

For Carly's class, Tattle Tail _____

_____

_____

Tattle Tail put his nose into the treat box. He grabbed three treats with his big buck teeth.

"You sneaky thief," Carly scolded. "It's all part of the act. My father filmed Tattle Tail's dance. We're going to enter the Funny Pet Contest. The winner will star on Animal TV and . . ."

Here Carly spotted The Joker grinning at her.

"And, and . . ." He kept on grinning. Carly felt flustered. She dropped the treat box. **5**

Stop and Think

5 How does Carly feel when The Joker grins at her? How can you tell?

When The Joker grins at her, Carly feels _____

_____

_____

Treats rolled everywhere. Tattle Tail was off in a flash. "Tattle Tail! That is not part of the act!" Carly went after her rabbit.

Tattle Tail ran in a zigzag. Then he made a flying leap. The rabbit landed on top of the row of sneakers. Tattle Tail sniffed the sneakers. Then he put both feet across his nose.

Carly's mouth froze open in surprise. She got a lump in her throat. Carly couldn't hear a sound from her class. **6**

Stop and Think

6 What does Tattle Tail do after he sniffs the sneakers?

After Tattle Tail sniffs the sneakers, he _____

_____

_____

A bubbly sound broke the quiet. Mrs. Fox started to laugh. A second later, the whole class started laughing. The Joker began to laugh the loudest.

"Thank you, Carly," Mrs. Fox said. "That was the best pet act I've ever seen. I believe Tattle Tail will win the Funny Pet Contest."

Carly petted Tattle Tail as her class left for lunch. "Mrs. Fox, that wasn't how Tattle Tail's act was supposed to end."

"I know, Carly. Sometimes the biggest surprises make the best acts." **7**

Stop and Think

7 Mrs. Fox says that the biggest surprises make the best acts. Why is this an opinion?

This is an opinion because _____

_____

Think Critically

1. What did Carly do after the rabbit got the spilled treats? Copy the chart, and fill it in. **CAUSE AND EFFECT**

Cause		Effect
Carly's rabbit got the spilled treats.	→	

2. Why do you think Carly taught Tattle Tail tricks? **CHARACTERS' MOTIVATIONS**

I think she taught him tricks because _____

_____

_____

3. What is the problem in the story? How is it solved? **PLOT**

The problem in the story is _____

_____

It is solved when _____

_____

Vocabulary

Build Robust Vocabulary

Write the word that best completes each sentence. The first one has been done for you.

1. A robot dog has an _____**ample**_____

ample   disgraceful   heroic

amount of tin, wire and screws.

2. One good thing about a robot dog is that

no food is _____ .

functional   visible   required

3. To be _____ ,

flustered   functional   ridiculous

a robot dog must have oil and not food.

4. One of April's _____ is to
inhabitants dialogues responsibilities
make sure the robot dog works well.

5. They are going to Tower Cliffs where
there are no _____ .
inhabitants swoops shelters
No one should be there.

6. Jack is in a state of _____ .
responsibility amazement emotion
A robot dog can drive a boat!

Write the answers to these questions. Use complete sentences.

7. What is required to make a robot dog functional?

_____

_____

8. What responsibilities does the robot dog have?

_____

_____

Leroy

by Nancy Furstinger
illustrated by Joe Lacey

CAST OF CHARACTERS

Narrator	Leroy
April	Tina
Jack	

Narrator: This story happens in 2050 aboard April's speedboat, the *Fortune*.

April: Ahoy, Jack! Look what I invented!

Jack: It looks like a toy dog.

April: This is Leroy, the world's first robot dog.

Leroy: Oink!

April: Well, I still have to work out some things. Why don't you join us aboard the *Fortune*?

Jack: Okay. I'm going to enjoy watching Leroy. **1**

Stop and Think

1 What is one thing about Leroy that April needs to fix?

One thing about Leroy that April needs to fix is

_____

_____

252

Jack: Why did you invent a toy, I mean, robot dog? Don't you think real dogs are good enough?

April: Leroy is better than a real dog.

Narrator: The robot dog fetches April's cowboy hat. Then he pretends to lick her hand.

Leroy: Leroy is loyal to April.

Jack: I don't know, April. Most real dogs have ample amounts of loyalty. Besides, a bunch of tin, wire, and screws just isn't the same as a real dog.

April: Wait, there's more. Tell him, Leroy.

Leroy: Leroy runs on oil. No food required.

Jack: That's very functional. Maybe a robot dog *would* make a good pet.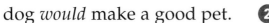

Stop and Think

❷ Why doesn't Leroy require dog food?

Leroy doesn't require dog food because _____

_____

_____

© Harcourt

April: Let's take a trip. I'll show you some more reasons that it's good to have a dog like Leroy.

Narrator: Leroy puts on a captain's hat and begins to steer the boat away from the dock.

Jack: I'm in a state of amazement! Can Leroy really control the boat?

Leroy: Leroy can control a whole fleet of boats.

April: I just punch in where we want to go. Watch this.

Narrator: April types in *"Tower Cliffs"* using a small keyboard on the robot dog's back.

Jack: Wow! I think other people might want to buy their own robot dog. We can make more of them. So, how much would we need to invest?

April: Let's work it out. ❸

Stop and Think

❸ After Leroy steers the boat away, what does April do?

After Leroy steers the boat away, April _____

_____

_____

254

Narrator: As April and Jack figure out how much a bunch of robot dogs would cost, the boat speeds up. Before long, the water is getting choppy.

Jack: Leroy! I'm getting seasick.

Narrator: Leroy slows the boat to a crawl. A few minutes later, the boat stops.

Jack: That's not Tower Cliffs, April. It's Rocky Bluff. I think Leroy sniffed out the wrong spot.

Leroy: Leroy made a mistake.

Narrator: Leroy turns the *Fortune* another way. Before long, they arrive at a second spot.

April: Leroy! This is Pebble Point.

Leroy: Oink! Leroy begs your pardon. **4**

Stop and Think

4 What happens before the *Fortune* gets to Pebble Point?

Before the "Fortune" gets to Pebble Point, _____

_____

_____

April: One of my responsibilities is to be sure that Leroy makes no mistakes. I need to fix him before we can make more robot dogs.

Jack: That's true. Let him have one more try.

Narrator: This time, the *Fortune* arrives at Tower Cliffs. They step onto the beach.

Jack: Well, we have finally arrived! I still prefer real dogs because—

April: Just watch the fancy tricks Leroy can do. Why he—

Jack: —they are full of surprises.

April: —can throw the ball *and* catch it! **5**

Stop and Think

5 What might happen if April starts making more robot dogs now?

If April starts making more robot dogs now, _____

_____

_____

Narrator: Leroy picks up the ball, but not with his mouth!

Leroy: Should Leroy throw right or left? Fast or slow? North or south?

Jack: How disappointing. This takes all the fun out of playing ball with a dog.

April: Leroy, just throw the ball and have fun!

Narrator: The dog throws the ball. Then he runs and makes a perfect catch.

Leroy: Exercise completed.

April: What's that noise? There are no inhabitants at this spot. There should be no one here.

Jack: I hear some yelling . . . and barking! **6**

Stop and Think

6 When he plays with a ball, how does Leroy compare to a real dog?

When Leroy plays with a ball, he _____

_____

_____

Narrator: A big dog runs up to April and Jack, wagging his tail. His owner is following behind. When the dog sees Leroy, he barks in surprise.

Tina: Hold on, Max. What are you barking at?

April: We were just playing a game of ball with my robot dog.

Jack: Actually Leroy was playing ball with himself. He's not much fun to play catch with.

Tina: Try it with Max. But you'll have to throw the ball for him.

Narrator: Max runs after the ball, and then drops it at Jack's feet. Before Jack can get the ball, Leroy picks it up.

April: Leroy, what are you doing?

Jack: Look! Leroy is going to throw the ball. Hey, when I get tired of throwing, Leroy can do it!

Tina: Hmmm, real or robot, these two dogs are very entertaining. **7**

Stop and Think

7 Would you like to play ball with a robot dog? Explain your answer.

I would _____

_____

_____

Think Critically

1. After Max drops the ball at Jack's feet, what does Leroy do?

SEQUENCE

After Max drops the ball at Jack's feet, Leroy

_____

_____

_____

2. What would you teach a robot dog to do? PERSONAL

RESPONSE

I would teach a robot dog to _____

_____

_____

_____

3. How does the play end? PLOT

At the end of the play, _____

_____

_____

_____

boasting

nuisance

oblige

sedentary

summoning

sway

Vocabulary

Build Robust Vocabulary

Write the Vocabulary Word that completes each sentence. The first one has been done for you.

Splash loved **(1)** _____**boasting**_____ that
he was the best. He was going to make the best
cookie for his pal. But he forgot how!

Splash wanted help. Anna said she would
(2) _____ him by helping him
make the cookie. Anna looked at her cookbook.
"Step one, gather goose eggs."

© Harcourt

Splash stepped into the goose hut. The **(3)** _____ goose was resting quietly in her nest. She would not move.

(4) _____ all his strength, Splash asked her to move. Then he picked up some eggs.

Some of the eggs cracked. What a **(5)** _____! Anna's pigtails began to **(6)** _____ back and forth as she shook her head.

Splash's Surprise

by Nancy Furstinger

illustrated by Maryn Roos

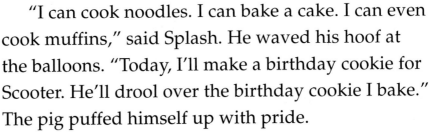

"I can cook noodles. I can bake a cake. I can even cook muffins," said Splash. He waved his hoof at the balloons. "Today, I'll make a birthday cookie for Scooter. He'll drool over the birthday cookie I bake." The pig puffed himself up with pride.

Anna let out a hoot. "When did you become a cook?" she asked.

Splash loved boasting. "I really like food. I'll bake that raccoon a cookie he'll never forget."

"Don't *you* forget!" Anna smiled with a laugh. "It's almost noon. The party's tonight. So you had better start cooking soon." ❶

Stop and Think

❶ Why is Splash baking a cookie for Scooter?

Splash is baking Scooter a cookie because _____

_____

_____

"Okay," Splash said. "Clear the room!"

"I'll be reading my book," said Anna.

Splash looked around. "Wait! I can't remember how to make my cookies!"

"Don't look so gloomy," Anna said. "I can help. Anything to oblige." Anna looked at her cookbook. "Step one, gather goose eggs."

"I'll be back," said Splash. He ran to the barn. **2**

Stop and Think

2 What is the first thing Splash needs for his cookie recipe?

The first thing Splash needs is _____

_____

_____

Splash stepped into the goose hut. The sedentary goose was in her nest, resting quietly. Summoning all of his pig strength, Splash asked her to move. Then he stood on tiptoe to reach into the nest for some eggs.

"Ah! There are good goose eggs in this nest." Splash smiled. He scooped the eggs into his basket.

"Oops!" Some of the eggs cracked. "What a nuisance! Good thing I brought my spoon." The pig mixed the eggs in the basket with his spoon as he ran back to the kitchen.

Anna looked at the goop in his basket.

"I jumped to step two. I just beat the eggs," Splash said.

"Step three," Anna said with a smile. "Add milk. Come on, Splash. Back to the barn we go!" **3**

Stop and Think

3 What are the next two steps for Splash's cookie recipe?

The next two steps for Splash's cookie recipe are _____

_____

_____

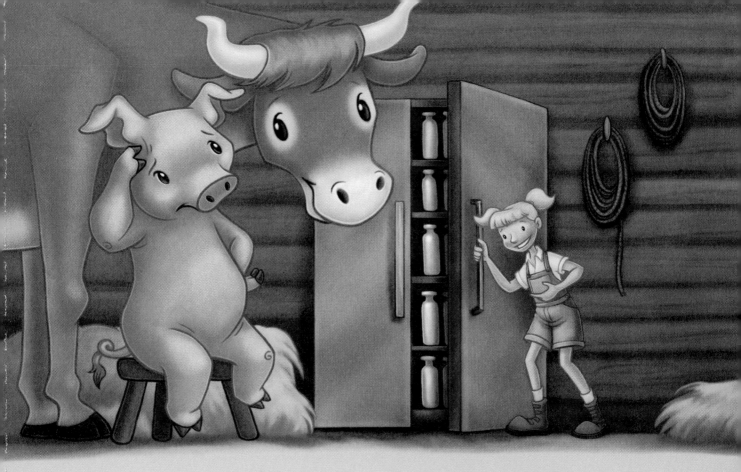

The cow called out a big moo as Splash sat on a stool. He didn't know what to do next. "Just how do I get milk from this cow?" he asked Anna.

"You could spend all afternoon learning how to milk a cow," Anna said. "Or you could just use the milk in the cooler."

Splash looked in the cooler. "Doesn't this milk come in different flavors? I want to make chocolate cookies. I just see white milk. Maybe I could stir in some mud." Splash swished his hoof in the mud. ④

Stop and Think

④ Why does Splash want to stir mud into the milk?

Splash wants to stir mud into the milk because _____

_____

_____

265

Anna hooted and chuckled until her pigtails began to sway back and forth. "There's no mud listed in my cookbook!" she giggled.

"Mud adds to the flavor of food!" he cried.

The pig looked through Anna's cookbook for Scooter's favorite foods. He mumbled, "What kind of cookbook is this? I don't see anything Scooter will like." Splash waved his spoon. "I shall invent my own recipe." **5**

Stop and Think

5 Do you think Splash is creative? Explain your answer.

I think Splash _____

_____

_____

Splash sent Anna out of the room to blow up more balloons. Soon, Anna heard a crash.

"Oh no!" cried Splash. "Help!"

Anna rushed into the room. Goop oozed from everywhere. It even dripped from Splash's nose to his feet.

"I'm doomed," Splash said. "I mixed together all of Scooter's favorite foods. How silly I am. I made goop, not cookies!" **6**

Stop and Think

6 What happens when Splash mixes together Scooter's favorite foods?

When Splash mixes together Scooter's favorite foods,

_____

_____

"Let's clean up this room," Anna said. "Then you can clean yourself up."

Splash returned, all cleaned up and in a good mood. "I have a plan," he said. "It popped into my brain when I was washing up. Do you know what I think Scooter's most favorite food is? Blueberry pancakes! Hand me my spoon."

Then Splash looked around at the now clean kitchen. "I have a better idea. Let's go somewhere with Scooter and order blueberry pancakes."

Anna smiled and gave the pig a big kiss on his snout. **7**

Stop and Think

7 What happens after Splash cleans up?

After Splash cleans up, he _____

_____

_____

© Harcourt

Think Critically

1. What happens in the story that shows Splash is not a very good cook? Copy the chart, and fill it in. PLOT

> **Splash brags about his cooking.**
>
> ↓
>
> **Splash makes up his own recipe.**
>
> ↓
>
> [ ]

2. Why does Anna give Splash a kiss at the end of the story? CHARACTERS

Anna gives Splash a kiss because _____

_____

_____

3. What do you think the author wants you to learn from this story? AUTHOR'S PURPOSE

I think the author wants me to learn _____

_____

_____

Vocabulary

prey

reels

shallow

social

spiral

strands

Build Robust Vocabulary

Write the Vocabulary Word that completes each sentence in the letters. The first one has been done for you.

Dear Mike,

This museum is amazing! I learned about wolf spiders. Some spiders have a **(1)** _____ spiral _____ web, but these don't. Wolf spiders don't wait for their food to come to a web. They chase their **(2)** _____ .

Mom got me a book about spiders. When I get back next week, I'll show it to you.

Your long legged friend,

Jim

Dear Shelley,

I'm at a spider show at the museum. I found out that trap-door spiders make nests in groups, but they prefer to be alone. They are not **(3)** _____ .

The trap-door spider lives under the soil. It digs a tube in the ground and lines it with **(4)** _____ of silk. Then it **(5)** _____ out more silk to make a flap at the entrance. It hides until an insect gets close then . . . WATCH OUT!

The one that got away,

Jim

Dear Carl,

I'm learning about spiders at the museum. Some are harmful to people, but a tarantula is not. It looks scary, but you can have one as a pet. You will need to give it a **(6)** _____ dish of water and something to eat. It also needs a place to hide.

Would you like me to bring you a tarantula for a pet? I'm just teasing!

Your friend,

Jim

Spiders Without Webs

by Ernest Kaye

When you think about spiders, do you picture one resting at the edge of a spiral web? For many spiders, a web is unnecessary. They may wait to ambush their prey. Others may race after what they want for a meal.

The Wolf Spider

Just like wolves, wolf spiders chase and pounce on their prey. That's how they get their name. Their hairy bodies are low to the ground so they look like they're always hunting. Thick legs help them move quickly. Sharp eyes also help. Two big eyes face forward while two others face up. Four smaller eyes are spaced in a row below the others. ❶

Stop and Think

❶ How does the wolf spider get its name?

The wolf spider gets its name because _____

_____

_____

Wolf spiders find places to live in tall grass or under stones, logs, or fallen leaves. In these places, they're certain to find insects. Only by accident do wolf spiders wander indoors, looking for a safe place in winter. You might find one in your cellar or attic.

The cycle of life begins when a female wolf spider lays her eggs. She places them in a giant sac. She balances the sac on her body until the eggs hatch. Then the baby spiders catch a ride on her back for several days. ❷

Stop and Think

❷ What happens after a female wolf spider lays her eggs?

After the female wolf spider lays her eggs, she _____

_____

_____

The Trap-Door Spider

Each trap-door spider nests beneath the surface of the soil. First, it digs a tube in the ground. Then, it reels out strands of silk that it uses to line the tube. The spider makes a fancy flap at the entrance. It hides and waits behind this flap. If it notices an insect close by, the spider springs out and catches it.

Except when hunting, trap-door spiders will stay inside their tube. They are timid and race back into the tube if frightened. Birds and other animals like to have these spiders as a meal. If a spider glances at an animal on the hunt, back into the tube it goes! ❸

Stop and Think

❸ Why does a trap-door spider make a flap for its tube?

A trap-door spider makes a flap so _____

_____

_____

Trap-door spiders have stocky bodies with short thick legs. They are somewhat shiny and have few hairs. Their eyes are close together, with a pair in the center and three to each side. Some trap-door spiders have rows of teeth for digging. All of them use their mouths to dig a tube. They lift the soil, roll it into a ball, and toss the ball out with their back legs.

The adult spiders most often make nests in groups, but they are not social. The spiders prefer to be alone, except for mother spiders. The babies hatch in the mother's tunnel. They remain in the tunnel for a few weeks. Then they decide on a place for a new tube of their own. **4**

Stop and Think

4 How many eyes does a trap-door spider have? Underline the words that tell you.

Trap-door spiders have _____

_____

_____

The Tarantula

Tarantulas are the largest spiders we know. Some live in deserts, but most live in rain forests. They may dig nests, or live under rocks or in holes. They hunt mostly at night, waiting for insects to wander by. These spiders can live up to twenty years.

Tarantulas are very hairy with thick, stocky bodies. Most are black or brown. A few have fancy colors, with stripes of bright red or blue on their legs.

You would not want to introduce your pet bird to a giant tarantula from South America. This bird-eating spider is very large. Including its legs, it can be up to 10 inches across! **5**

Stop and Think

5 Why does the author tell you not to introduce your pet bird to a giant tarantula?

The author tells me not to because _____

_____

_____

The poison produced by tarantulas isn't harmful to us. But their bite can still be painful. These spiders look frightening but will race away rather than fight. If trapped, tarantulas may stand on their back legs, show their fangs, and prepare to strike. Some make a hissing sound by rubbing their legs together. Others throw hairs at enemies. These hairs produce rashes.

Not many enemies will try to catch such a large spider, except for humans. In some places, humans eat roasted tarantulas for lunch! **6**

Stop and Think

6 What would you do if someone offered you a roasted tarantula for lunch?

I would _____

_____

_____

Spiders look scary. And some spiders are harmful to people. But there is no need to be afraid of the wolf spider, trap-door spider, or tarantula! These spiders are not harmful to us. They would rather run away than bite.

In fact, these spiders are helpful. They eat insects that bother us or damage our plants. We need them to control many insect pests.

How about a spider as a pet? Tarantulas are quiet and take up little space. They need a place to hide and a shallow dish of water. They also need something to eat. A cricket a week is enough. After a while, you may learn a lot more about spiders! **7**

Stop and Think

7 The author states that "spiders look scary." Is this a fact or opinion? How can you tell?

"Spiders look scary" is _____

_____

_____

Think Critically

1. What have you learned about spiders? Copy the chart, and fill it in. MAKE INFERENCES

What You Know

A spider can be a pet.

What the Author Tells You

Inference

A pet tarantula helps you learn about spiders.

2. How can you tell that trap-door spiders like to be alone? DRAW CONCLUSIONS

I can tell this because _____

_____

3. Why might you find a wolf spider in your cellar or attic? CAUSE AND EFFECT

I might find a wolf spider there because

_____

_____

deliberation

erupt

expand

grainy

sprinkled

thorough

Vocabulary

Build Robust Vocabulary

Write the Vocabulary Word that completes each sentence in the diary. The first one has been done for you.

Sunday, September 10th

 Art and I spent a lot of time thinking about the science fair. We had to come up with a good idea. After much **(1)** _____**deliberation**_____, we decided what to do. It's top secret for now.

 We have to get everything right. We have to be

(2) _____ and cover all the facts when we explain it at the science fair. I want to win!

 Today Art called and told me about one of the other projects. It sounds really good. It's a volcano that will

(3) _____ . I'm not sure if we can beat that. We'll see!

280

© Harcourt

Monday, September 11th

    We just finished setting up our science fair project in the gym. I can see the other kids setting their projects up, too. I feel awful. I don't think we're going to win.

    This morning, I saw April and Dawn walking to the bus stop. They had small race cars and some kind of model habitat. The habitat was **(4)** _____ with real grass.

    My throat feels dry. I tried to eat a small bite of chocolate. It tastes **(5)** _____ , like sawdust and sand. I don't think our project is so terrific now. We're supposed to show how heat makes chocolate **(6)** _____ and become a liquid as it spreads out. Who wants to know about that!

Our Science Project

by Nancy Furstinger
illustrated by Laura Freeman

I woke up, yawning widely. Then I remembered. Today was the first science fair at school.

My cat poked me with her paw. She meowed until I rolled out of bed.

"What if I make a mistake?" I asked my cat.

I thought about the science fair. In my mind, I saw a thousand mistakes that we could easily make. "What if our project is awful? What if Mrs. Shaw is just saying she thinks we have a chance to win? What if I forget what Art taught me?"

My cat just yawned. ❶

Stop and Think

❶ How does Rose feel when she wakes up? How can you tell?

Rose feels _____

_____

_____

Later, on the bus, I saw April and Dawn. Checkered flags, toy race cars, and tracks spilled out of a box that Dawn held.

"Our race car track will be the best," said Dawn.

"You've never seen an experiment like this, Rose," April told me. "And Ryan and Lon will set up their animal habitat at the fair. You know, the one that shows where an animal lives. If I know that team, their project will be flawless." Ryan and Lon knew their stuff.

I felt like crying. Suddenly, our project didn't sound so fantastic. **2**

Stop and Think

2 What happens that makes Rose think her project isn't so fantastic?

Rose doesn't think her project is so fantastic because

_____

_____

I headed to the gym. I paused before going inside. I worried, but I really wanted us to win!

"Over here, Rose!" Art caught my eye. "I just have to haul in one more box," he said.

After much deliberation, I decided where to hang our posters. Then Art and I set up our project.

I stared at the project across from us. Will and Chip had a model of an astronaut's suit. Their labels and note cards were thorough and easy to understand. I was awestruck!

Stop and Think

3 Do you think that Rose and Art have a chance to win? Explain.

I think Rose and Art _____

_____

_____

© Harcourt

"Look at that! Maybe we should withdraw."

"Oh, it's okay!" Art said. "Our science project is—"

I didn't wait to hear him finish. I dashed around the gym, pausing at each project to see what the others had done.

I watched as the race car track began to fill up one table. The habitat, sprinkled with real grass, also looked grand. There was even a volcano model that was all set up to erupt. All three projects made me want to crawl into a hole somewhere. I felt awful. I almost hid under our table. Then I saw Mrs. Shaw coming our way. **4**

Stop and Think

4 From whose point of view is the story told? How can you tell?

The story is told from _____

_____

_____

The judges caught up to her. And behind them, I saw my parents. I saw Art's parents, too.

"Hello, Rose and Art. Why don't you tell us about your project?" Mrs. Shaw asked.

Art was ready. "We're going to show how solids can became liquids," he explained. Then he started the experiment. He explained how the heat from the lamp made the chocolate melt. "Now it is a liquid. As the heat turns it into a liquid, it expands."

There was an awkward pause. It was my turn. Art bumped me under the table. **5**

Stop and Think

5 What happens after Art puts the chocolate under the lamp?

After Art puts the chocolate under the lamp, _____

_____

_____

I cleared my throat. "Now we'll show how liquids can become solids," I said, shaking. I explained how the ice cooled the liquid, changing the melted chocolate back into a solid.

"I see," Mrs. Shaw said. I saw the judges drawing on their charts. They moved to the next project.

"We were awesome!" Art exclaimed. I didn't feel awesome. I was still shaking. I chewed on some chocolate. It tasted grainy, like sawdust. **6**

Stop and Think

6 The experiment is a success. Why doesn't Rose feel awesome?

Rose doesn't feel awesome because _____

_____

_____

I caught Dawn's eye. "How did your race car experiment go?"

"Well," Dawn giggled, "it was fine until the track fell. That launched a race car into space!"

I tried not to giggle. But Dawn seemed to take this mistake pretty well.

Then it was time for the awards. Mrs. Shaw announced second prize. Ryan and Lon won.

I thought that we were doomed. Suddenly, the room filled with cheers. "We won!" Art shouted.

Art and I made our way up to the stage. I had to admit, "I guess we really were awesome after all!" **7**

Stop and Think

7 Tell about a time when you thought something didn't go well, only to discover that it went very well after all.

There was a time when _____

_____

_____

Think Critically

1. What happens during the award ceremony? Copy the chart, and fill it in. SEQUENCE

> Mrs. Shaw announces the winners.

↓

>

↓

>

2. What problem does Rose have in the story? How is the problem solved? PLOT

Rose's problem is that _____

_____

_____

_____

3. What lesson does the author want you to learn from this story? AUTHOR'S PURPOSE

The author wants me to learn _____

_____

_____

© Harcourt

appears

evidence

reflects

rotates

steady

surface

Vocabulary

Build Robust Vocabulary

Write the Vocabulary Word that completes each sentence in the selection. The first one has been done for you.

The Moon is the second brightest object that

(1) _____appears_____ in our sky. The Moon has no

light of its own. It only **(2)** _____ light

from the Sun. This happens when the Sun's light hits the

Moon's **(3)** _____ .

The Moon travels around Earth. It takes about one month for this to happen. From Earth, the Moon looks different each day. That's because we see only part of the light that hits the Moon.

Long ago, meteorites kept hitting the Moon. Their **(4)** _____ collisions made holes on the Moon that look like bowls. These holes are called *craters*.

As the Moon travels around Earth, it also spins around, or **(5)** _____ . We see the same side of the Moon each month. During a full moon, look at its craters. When the next full moon comes, look again. You'll see the same craters. This **(6)** _____ tells us something about the Moon. It is proof that one rotation also happens in about one month.

The Moon

by Ernest Kaye

illustrated by Mike Maydek

What do you know about the Moon? When it's full, do you see a man in the Moon? Did you ever hear that the Moon was made of cheese? Do animals really howl at the Moon? Do you? The Moon is the second brightest object that appears in our sky. Only the Sun is brighter. But the Moon reflects light. It has no light of its own. ❶

Waxing Gibbous

First Quarter

Waxing Crescent

New Moon

Stop and Think

❶ What do you think you will learn about the Moon in this selection?

I think I will learn _____

_____

_____

The Moon's Stages

The Moon revolves around Earth. It takes about one month for it to make the trip around our planet. As it circles around us, it looks different as each day goes by. When it begins its trip around Earth, it is called a new moon. A new moon is almost invisible. In the middle of its trip, we see a full moon. A full moon is a bright circle of light.

Remember how the Moon only reflects sunlight? During a new moon, no light is reflected. During a full moon, a full side of the Moon reflects light back to Earth. **2**

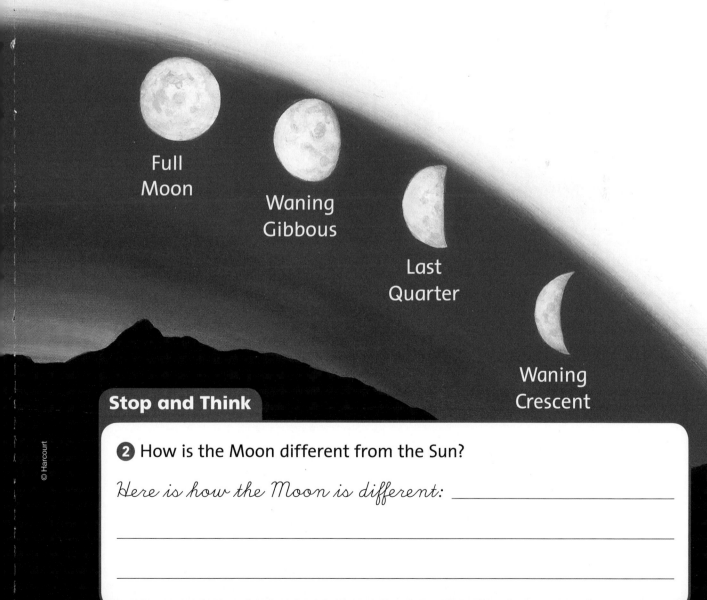

Full Moon

Waning Gibbous

Last Quarter

Waning Crescent

Stop and Think

2 How is the Moon different from the Sun?

Here is how the Moon is different: _____

_____

_____

The Moon's Beginning

Scientists once wrongly believed the Moon split off from Earth. Now they know that Earth crashed into some object long ago. From the broken bits of this wreck, the Moon formed.

Scientists have studied rocks from the Moon. This evidence gave us clues about the Moon's age. We now know that some rocks are more than four billion years old! **3**

Stop and Think

3 What have scientists learned from studying Moon rocks?

From studying Moon rocks, scientists have learned

The Moon's Surface

Do you know that the Moon is covered with craters? Its surface looks like it has been poked with giant knitting needles!

For billions of years, meteorites crashed into the Moon. Their steady collisions made the craters. The smallest craters are as tiny as the tip of a knife. The largest are as wide as the United States! ❹

Stop and Think

❹ Why does the Moon have craters on its surface?

The Moon has craters on its surface because _____

_____

_____

The Moon and the Tides

Do you know that tides are caused by the Moon? Tides are the rising and falling of the oceans' water levels. Tides happen because of the pull of gravity between Earth and the Moon.

Water bulges out as Earth and the Moon pull at each other. The seas on both sides of Earth bulge. Since Earth rotates, two tides happen each day.

If you think Earth's pull causes tides on the Moon, you would be wrong. No liquid water is on the Moon. There is no water to pull! ⑤

Stop and Think

⑤ What happens after Earth and the Moon pull at each other?

After Earth and the Moon pull at each other, _____

_____

_____

Studying the Moon

Did you know that the Moon is the only place in space that humans have visited? The first rocket went to the Moon in 1959. It took pictures of the back side of the Moon.

Humans did not set foot on the Moon until 1969. We collected rock and soil samples to study. Since then, people have gone to the Moon many times. From these trips, we now know more about the Moon. **6**

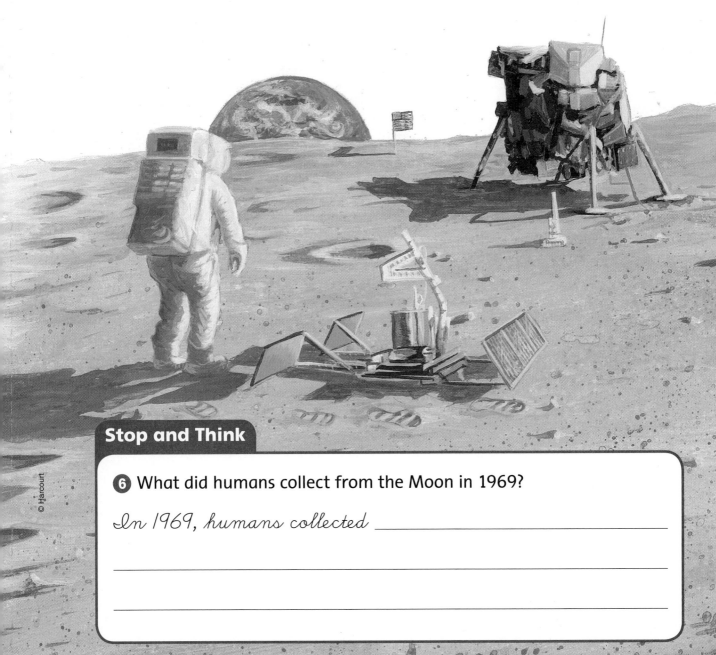

Stop and Think

6 What did humans collect from the Moon in 1969?

In 1969, humans collected _____

_____

_____

What will happen next with Moon travel? Some people write about an outpost, or settlement, on the Moon. They think it might be a good place to find minerals. Others think the Moon might be a good stopping point between Earth and the other planets.

We can use what we know about the Moon to make a place for humans to live there. Just think, maybe your children or their children will live on the Moon some day! **7**

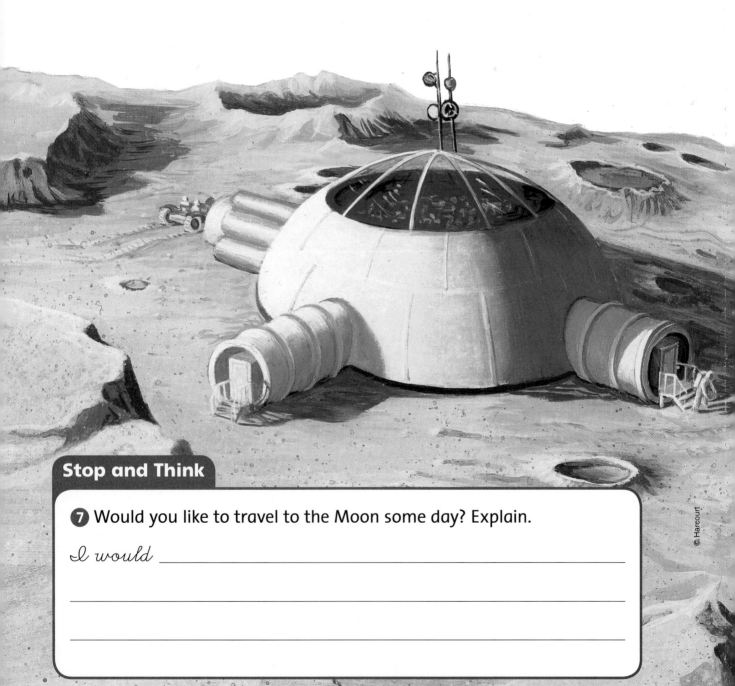

Stop and Think

7 Would you like to travel to the Moon some day? Explain.

I would _____

_____

_____

Think Critically

1. What did you learn about the Moon? Copy the chart, and fill it in. **MAIN IDEA AND DETAILS**

Moon Facts	Moon Travel	Moon's Future
The Moon revolves around Earth.		

2. Why doesn't Earth's pull cause tides on the Moon? **CAUSE AND EFFECT**

   Earth's pull doesn't cause tides on the Moon because _____

   _____

   _____

3. What does the author want you to learn from this selection? **AUTHOR'S PURPOSE**

   The author wants me to learn _____

   _____

   _____

Vocabulary

Build Robust Vocabulary

Write the word that best completes each sentence. The first one has been done for you.

1. If Josh's parrot is ____**observed**____ on

safeguard   observed   spiral

board the ship, it'll be a catastrophe.

2. Captain Woods hears a strange squawk.

He wants to _____ that it isn't

confirm   oblige   remark

a real problem.

3. Ginger asks how they cook in space.

A space stove _____

generates   safeguards   rotates

heat to cook on the ship.

4. Josh wants to see the space house. It has a

special cloth to _____

              magnify   erupt   safeguard

people from danger.

5. Telescopes _____ things

          confirm   magnify   clutter

when you look through them. Josh uses one

to look at the planet's surface.

6. The kids see some incredible views. Mars is

such a _____ planet.

    picturesque   steady   grainy

Write the answers to these questions. Use complete sentences.

7. What does Josh observe in the telescope?

_____

_____

8. If something is picturesque, what is it like?

_____

_____

Trip to Mars

by Nancy Furstinger
illustrated by Larry Moore

Cast of Characters

Josh · · · · · · · · · · · · Ginger
Captain Woods · · · · · · Dr. Ling
Pepper

Josh: I still can't believe we're riding aboard a spaceship to Mars!

Ginger: What's it called again?

Josh: The *Sphinx.*

Ginger: It was tough getting my parents to let me go on this trip, even if your uncle is the captain.

Pepper: Awk! Warning! Humans are coming!

Josh: Quick, Pepper, hide! My uncle may not like it if he discovers you on board. **1**

Stop and Think

1 Why does Pepper give a warning squawk?

Pepper gives a warning squawk because _____

_____

_____

Ginger: Pepper is right though. I hear them.

Josh: It'll be a catastrophe if my parrot is observed on board.

Ginger: Why? Doesn't your uncle like Pepper?

Josh: He likes Pepper. But he may not think Pepper belongs on a spaceship. Just in case, let's hide him behind these boards.

Ginger: What are these boards? They feel like they're made of cellophane.

Josh: They're made from a new fabric that Dr. Ling invented. When the boards are filled with air, they form walls for a space house. **2**

Stop and Think

2 What will happen after the boards are filled with air?

After the boards are filled with air, they _____

_____

_____

Captain Woods: Did I just hear a squawk?

Dr. Ling: It was most likely a gear that needs to be oiled. I can confirm that there is no real problem.

Captain Woods: I'm not so sure, Dr. Ling. It sounded like my nephew's parrot. A bird on the spaceship was not in my plans.

Dr. Ling: Isn't that the bird that repeats the alphabet when he gets upset or worried?

Pepper: A, B, C, D, . . .

Captain Woods: Pepper! Why are you here?

Josh: Sorry, it's my fault. Pepper just wanted to be the first bird on Mars. ❸

Stop and Think

❸ What happens when Pepper recites the alphabet?

When Pepper recites the alphabet, _____

_____

_____

Captain Woods: Well, it looks as if Pepper will get his wish.

Ginger: Captain Woods, thank you for inviting me on this trip to the Red Planet.

Josh: Why is Mars called the Red Planet?

Dr. Ling: Have you ever seen how it glows fiery red in the night sky?

Josh: Yes, in photographs. It looks like a bright red disk. But why is it red?

Captain Woods: We believe the color is caused by iron-rich dust on the surface. How about some lunch?

Ginger: How are we going to cook things?

Dr. Ling: We have a space stove that generates heat without a flame. It's safe enough to use in space. How about some alphabet soup?

Josh: How appropriate for Pepper!

Pepper: Awk! Don't forget the crackers. ❹

Stop and Think

❹ Why does Mars appear red in photographs?

Mars appears red because _____

_____

_____

Dr. Ling: What would you think about a vacation house on Mars, Ginger?

Ginger: It's a long trip to travel from Earth for a vacation.

Josh: I saw the photos in your pamphlet about the space house you invented, Dr. Ling. I wondered if you and my uncle might try to settle on Mars.

Dr. Ling: Ever since I was a boy, I thought it would be interesting to live on another planet.

Captain Woods: Dr. Ling's space house would make it possible. It has a special cloth to safeguard people from the dangers of the planet's rough geography and atmosphere. It was first tested at the South Pole! **5**

Stop and Think

5 Why do you think Dr. Ling is taking his space house to Mars?

I think he is taking his space house to Mars because

_____

_____

© Harcourt

Ginger: Can we look closer at Mars through the *Sphinx's* telescopes?

Dr. Ling: Certainly. They magnify the planet's surface to help you see it better.

Josh: Mars is such a picturesque planet. Look, this view is incredible! I can see a huge mountain.

Ginger: It's called Olympus Mons. It's more than twice as high as the largest mountain on our planet!

Captain Woods: And there are polar caps at the north and south poles of Mars.

Josh: Look! Mars has two moons!

Ginger: They're named after the horses of the Greek god of war.

Dr. Ling: That's right. 6

Stop and Think

6 Why are telescopes important for a spaceship to carry?

Telescopes are important for a spaceship to carry because

_____

_____

Captain Woods: Buckle up, everyone.

Josh: What a triumph! Soon we'll be the first humans to walk on Mars!

Pepper: And the first bird to fly there!

Ginger: Do you think there is life on Mars?

Dr. Ling: It's possible. Perhaps we'll find simple life forms underground, where some scientists think water flows.

Captain Woods: Our trip to Mars could answer that question. Are you ready?

Josh and Ginger: Yes! Let's make history!

Pepper: Count me in. Awk! ⑦

Stop and Think

⑦ What do you think will happen after the *Sphinx* lands on Mars?

I think that after the "Sphinx" lands on Mars, _____

_____

_____

Think Critically

1. Why will the crew aboard the *Sphinx* make history? **MAKE INFERENCES**

   The crew aboard the "Sphinx" will make history because _____

   _____

2. Why might the space house be good for Mars's rough geography and atmosphere? **MAIN IDEA AND DETAILS**

   The space house might be good for Mars's rough geography and atmosphere because _____

   _____

   _____

3. Why do you think the author includes facts about Mars in this play? **AUTHOR'S PURPOSE**

   I think the author includes facts about Mars so _____

   _____

   _____